Religious Education at a Crossroads

Moving On in the Freedom of the Spirit

Francoise Darcy-Berube

Foreword by Thomas H. Groome

PAULIST PRESS
New York • Mahwah

Cover art courtesy of Scala/Art Resource, NY

Library of Congress Cataloging-in-Publication Data

Darcy-Berube, Francoise.
    Religious education at a crossroads : moving on in the freedom of the Spirit / Francoise Darcy-Berube ; foreword by Thomas H. Groome.
        p. cm.
    Includes bibliographical references.
    ISBN 0-8091-0476-8 (alk. paper)
        1. Christian education—Philosophy.   2. Catholic Church—Education.
    3. Darcy-Berube, Francoise.   I. Title.
    BX926.D37   1995
    268'.82—dc20   95-22291
                                                                            CIP

Published by Paulist Press
997 Macarthur Boulevard
Mahwah, New Jersey 07430

Printed and bound in the
United States of America

Contents

Part One: General Perspectives

Part Two: Practical Applications

Part Three: Awakenings: The Unique Importance of the Beginnings

Dedication

In spite of its title this is not a "radical" book. Neither is it an academic book. It is a very simple book, something like conversations among friends who have for many years tried to share their faith with others and who sit together for a leisurely day, sharing memories, observations, questions and dreams.

It is also a grateful book. I dedicate it to the innumerable people who have over some forty-five years and in four different countries graced me with the sharing of their faith, of their life, of their ideas. These were mostly children and young people from pre-school to university, but also parents, teachers, pastoral ministers and colleagues. Meeting them, working with them, learning from them, sharing with them the wonders of our faith, has been and is still the joy of my life. Indeed many of the ideas in this book were born and nourished in my heart and mind through such conversations; so this book is theirs as much as mine.

Acknowledgments

If this book has finally come to be it is thanks to Father Kevin Lynch, President of Paulist Press, who has been asking me to write it for many years. But I owe much more than that to Father Lynch. He was the one who introduced me—if I might say—to one of the great loves of my life: the United States of America! It was when I began flying around this country with Kevin, giving workshops on *Come to the Father* from New Jersey to California, that I discovered the stunning beauty and diversity of America, the vibrant vitality, the intelligence, friendliness, dedication and free spirit of its people. My love for this country has never faltered even in discovering over the years, as in all relationships, that it also had a few shortcomings! So I am deeply indebted to Father Lynch who, throughout his remarkable career at the helm of Paulist Press, has remained a very caring friend both to me and to my husband John-Paul.

Concerning John-Paul I would like to say this: whatever wisdom there might be in this book, it is the fruit of the work, and later on the life and love I was blessed to share with him for more than thirty years. All along those years we have tried together, in our teaching and writing, to be attentive both to the signs of the time and to the moves of the Spirit. We chose to concentrate our efforts especially on helping young children and their parents discover and enjoy the wonders of God's love in their hearts and their lives, and we are happy we were able to do our small share in this unending mission of the Church.

I would also like to express my warm gratitude to my friend

and former student Thomas Groome who encouraged me from the start to write this book and who so kindly offered to help in any way he could. As you will see I gladly took advantage of this gracious offer in several ways and benefitted greatly from his very wise suggestions on how to improve the manuscript. I find it very touching that Tom thus helped his old professor with one of her last contributions to catechetics in America, because, as Tom recalls in the Foreword, I had the privilege to give him his first opportunity to speak publicly in this country twenty-two years ago. I knew from experience that he was bright, dedicated, hard-working, and that he had the special Irish charm, warmth and humor which would make him very successful in religious education; that is why I wanted to give him a chance to start using his gifts right away. But how amazingly he has surpassed even the great hopes I had for him!

Finally, I would also like to thank my editor Dennis McManus. It was wonderful working with him because he understands what you want to say even before you have finished your sentence! His encouragement and wise counsel, his dedication to help, his patience and sense of humor made it a real pleasure to cooperate with him.

Foreword: Wisdom from the Heat of the Day

By THOMAS H. GROOME

The Good Book says that those who come at the eleventh hour shall also be entitled to "the penny." However, in my human sense of justice, I always have a feeling of fealty toward those who have borne the heat of the day. Among other things, they are likely to have some hard won wisdom that the rest of us would be foolish to forget.

This seems eminently appropriate in the field of religious education and the ministry of catechesis. No one will dispute that this is a challenging enterprise; enough to survive in it, but to thrive in it for a long public career is surely a miracle of God's grace writ large. Those who achieve this difficult feat have much from the heat of the day to teach the rest who "come later." Such a person is Francoise Darcy-Berube. And in this small book she gathers together for us her hard-won wisdom from a lifetime in catechetics.

Francoise Darcy-Berube was born in Paris, and spent some early childhood years in England. As an undergraduate she studied psychology at La Sorbonne and L'Institut Catholique in Paris, and was very active in the Young Catholic Student Action movement. Thereafter she went on and graduated from the Lumen Vitae Catechetical Institute in Brussels. A 1961 essay in *Lumen Vitae* on curriculum design brought her international attention and an invitation to join a writing team in Quebec beginning to work on a new curriculum. Among others on that team was her future husband

John-Paul Berube; thereafter much of her writing has been in partnership with her beloved John-Paul. She continued her studies in
Canada and received a Master's degree from Montreal University,
and a Doctorate from the University of Ottawa.

Francoise is truly one of the great "mothers" of contemporary
Catholic catechetics. With a handful of other pioneers, she laid the
foundations and helped to forge the paradigm shift in religious
education that has emerged over the past fifty years. As a young
woman in Paris and Brussels, she experienced first-hand the heady
ferment of the early catechetical movement that later received official benediction at Vatican II. A truly multi-cultural and "international" person, throughout her life she has continued to create
and facilitate the dialogue between European and North American
catechists, drawing from and sharing insights on both sides of the
Atlantic, and on both sides of the U.S. and Canadian border.

Her most significant early contribution was as a primary au-
thor of the *Come to the Father* (in Canada: *The Canadian Catechism*) religion curriculum (from Paulist Press, 1967). This was a
most significant breakthrough in contemporary catechesis in North
America. With the *On Our Way* series from W. H. Sadlier, *Come
to the Father* brought the first fruits of catechetical renewal into the
textbooks of American Catholic children. Thereafter, through her
teaching in many Catholic universities, her frequent traveling for
conferences and conventions, her curriculum work, and her professional writings, she has been a major presence and force for
renewal in the catechetical ministry of the Church.

Francoise Darcy-Berube has helped to create and establish
many of the things that we now take for granted as integral to
good pastoral catechesis. At the top of the list I would place her
work to establish a Trinitarian focus in catechesis (now a central
emphasis of the *Catechism of the Catholic Church*), and for young
children she based this catechesis more on their experience of
God's triune outreach and presence in their lives than on knowing

about the doctrinal mystery. Beyond that, she championed and helped to establish: the participation of parents in the sacramental preparation of their children, family and early childhood catechesis, the partnership of liturgy and catechesis, religious ritual to nurture the Christian formation of children, engaging and encouraging the contemplative capacity of the young child, the centrality of biblical and liturgical language in catechesis, and so on.

What has inspired this book? First, the urging of friends—myself among them—to review and glean from her long career some of her best wisdom for the rest of us. Not that her career is ending—far from it—but after some fifty years in this ministry, she is at that milestone in life when length and breadth of view and the clarity of hindsight give her "20/20" vision for the future. As she writes herself, "one of the many privileges of old age is that while feeling in our bones the weight of the past, we also carry in our heart and our mind all its riches." So she writes a lovely book, "something like conversations among friends who have for many years tried to share their faith with others. . . ."

But beyond this, she also writes because of a well-founded concern. She sees signs that some of the hard-won achievements of the catechetical renewal are being seriously threatened, and rather than continuing to build upon this legacy, we may lose ground. A particular symbol of her concern is the *Catechism of the Catholic Church.* Not that the Catechism in and of itself necessarily means catechetical retrenchment, but Francoise has compelling fears that it might be so abused, especially if it is used to focus exclusive attention again on "content" and "instruction"—both narrowly defined.

What will you find here? In gist, "vintage Francoise" that, like a good wine, has fermented and matured with the years. More specifically, and as the title suggests, you will find her response to her perception that the whole catechetical enterprise of Catholicism is "at a Crossroads." At this juncture, she believes, we have a choice either to *build upon* or to *abandon* "the paradigm shift" that has taken place in catechetics over her lifetime; she argues persuasively and passionately on behalf of continuing to build.

She describes the new paradigm as "a more holistic vision of religious education and a more pastoral approach to it." Gleaning from throughout the work, some features of this paradigm include:

- a catechesis for God's Reign of fullness of life for all, here and hereafter,
- educating and nurturing for lived Christian faith in every aspect and on every level of people's lives,
- actively engaging the shared life of the whole faith community to nurture the Christian identity of its members and its own renewal,
- being thoroughly aware of and taking into account the social context and psychological development of participants,
- addressing and engaging people's lives, their real interests and spiritual needs,
- honoring with great care and faithfulness the "faith handed on,"
- engaging people as active and constructive participants in the teaching/learning dynamic,
- creating conversations and learning communities in which the catechetical dynamic honors people's own lives and existential reality, gives them access to the rich legacy of scripture and Christian tradition, and enables them to appropriate and make "the faith" their own in the context of their lives in the world.

Beyond making a strong brief for this paradigm, she adds clarity and depth to it, with very practical suggestions for its pastoral realization.

Two words came to mind to describe the manuscript after reading it—*inspiring* and *balanced;* and I should note that I read it in the dim light and cold days of January when despair and excess come easily. I was inspired by the deep faith, warm passion, and enduring commitment that it reflects from the heart of this great woman. Throughout, Francoise herself shines through as a noble model, an elegant (as always) exemplar for all who dedicate themselves to this so significant and privileged ministry of "sharing faith." And it is a very balanced statement. For example, on the controversial issue of "religious literacy" she weaves her way carefully between the extremes of those who make it their "dominant preoccupation" and those who consider it "irrelevant and outmoded." Instead, she presents "a middle of the road view on the question" and proceeds to make some very helpful clarifications that might actually help both extremes to talk to each other again. This is typical of her!

How to read it? Ideally, my counsel is neither to rush it nor to read it alone. Instead, try to read it reflectively, allowing it to bring your own "praxis" into view and to enter into dialogue with the text, taking time to digest it, to come to new insights and renewed commitment. In sum, honor a perennial theme in her work throughout her public career and read it in a contemplative mode. And, if you can manage it at all, encourage a friend or colleagues to read it at the same time, and have conversations around its chapters and themes.

To encourage a contemplative and conversational reading, I offer, at Francoise's gracious invitation, a series of reflective questions at the beginning and end of each chapter. Astute readers will recognize that the opening statement and questions are resonant with the focusing activity and movements one and two of a shared praxis approach, and the closing questions reflect the intent of movements four and five. These questions are only to stimulate your own personal engagement with the text; likely you will often think of better ones.

It is not only an honor for me to participate with Francoise in bringing this book to publication, but also a pleasure because it gives me an opportunity to repay an old debt (though her graciousness, I'm sure, has long since canceled it). Francoise was one

of my professors during my Master's studies in religious education
at Fordham University, but here I have in mind something more
particular than the debt a student always owes to such a fine men-
tor and true "professor." In the spring of 1973, and before I had
even begun doctoral work in religious education, Francoise was
instrumental in having me invited to be a keynote presenter with
her at the annual catechetical congress of the Diocese of Altoona-
Johnstown, PA. I remember well the excitement of flying out with
her on my first big foray into the public forum of the catechetical
world. In gist, Francoise gave me "my first break"!

Francoise describes this work as "a grateful book," reflecting
her own gratitude for a long and rich ministry in catechetics. Over
the years, many of us have been grateful to her for many things,
and now for drawing together her wisdom from both "the heat of
the day" and "the cool of the evening."

Introduction

It seems to me that religious education in the U.S. finds itself at a dangerous crossroads. On the one hand, a slow and very creative paradigmatic shift has been taking shape in the last ten years and is now reaching a point where we can begin naming it with some precision. On the other hand, the Vatican has just published a catechism of the Catholic Church which Pope John Paul describes as "a valuable and authorized instrument at the service of the ecclesial community and a sure and certain standard for the teaching of the Church."

The danger of the publication of the Catechism at this time lies in the fact that it might refocus our attention mainly on the content and on the instructional aspect of religious education, bringing back orthodoxy and completeness as the main concern of curriculum design. Indeed, some people see the Document as a "catechetical messiah" which will solve all our problems: "Just teach everything that is in there, and all will be well!" However, I believe the Catechism of the Catholic Church can indeed be of help in inviting us to reflect on and discuss our Catholic Tradition in a more comprehensive way, provided we continue to move in the direction of the paradigmatic shift I mentioned. There is a tremendous power for renewal in this country. Will the publication of the Catechism break it or boost it? All will depend on the way we use it.

Many very competent people have begun and will continue writing about the Catechism, analyzing its strengths and shortcomings and describing ways it should be used or might be misused. What I will try to do in this book is describe in the simplest possible way what the paradigmatic shift we are experiencing is about and what wonderful potential it has for the renewal of religious education and of Christian life itself.

Before trying to make my point however, let me include a personal note. At the time of my busiest involvement in religious education, when I was all at once teaching, writing and lecturing around Canada and the U.S.A., I was flying away so often that a little friend of mine, a six year old neighbor, grew concerned about my life-style. So one day he asked me: "Tell me, why do you go away all the time for two or three days? Is it for work or for play?" So I tried to explain that I was going to various cities to speak to people. He got his own picture of my life and said: "Oh I see! You don't work, you just talk!"

The point I want to make is that this *"flying-around"* and this sharing with so many people has been, over the years, building up in me an increasingly strong and genuine admiration for and trust in the religious education community in this country. I do not mean that I admire everything that is being done in religious education as will become clear later. But I mean there is in the people of this community a vitality, an intelligence, a creativity, a generosity and a dedication which comprise a tremendous hope for the future. Of course, a paradigmatic shift always brings about a somewhat chaotic and confusing situation for a time. But I believe the Spirit of God has a kind of inclination to work wonders out of chaos! This, it seems to me, is exactly what She[1] is quietly doing in these troubled times. What we need then to cooperate with this mysterious work of the Spirit is the imagination, the will and the passion to find ways to bring all those tremendous energies to cooperate organically with one another on behalf of the Reign of God. We can then create together a total environment that will be conducive to the awakening, growth and progressive maturing of faith.

Having briefly stated the purpose of this book in the present context, let me explain how I intend to deal with it. I will not discuss theories. I will attempt rather to bring some clarity to the present situation in a pragmatic and operational way. I will try to pick out some of the more relevant aspects of the major trends of the day to see if we can bring them to some kind of organic interaction which could inspire and shape our search for renewal and excellence in religious education. In doing so, I will also have to critique other aspects of those trends which I feel might be detrimental to our search. I will try to do it in a respectful and friendly way even if I do it with passion!

PART ONE

GENERAL PERSPECTIVES

❖

Chapter One

The Rich Legacy of the Past

Focus for Reflection

It was from the ancient Hebrews that Christians first learned the importance of "remembering." They knew well that it was imperative to "remember"—especially what God had done for them—if they were to live faithfully as God's own people. Remembering helps us to stay the journey with right direction; forgetting is a sure means of losing one's way. Surely Jesus was speaking out of this Hebrew appreciation for memory when he said to disciples: "Do this in memory of me." Lest we forget!

- *Take a "flip" through a contemporary children's curriculum. Then, if you have it available, do the same with a traditional catechism; if not, recall the catechism of your childhood—or the question and answer one your parents told you about.*

- *What are some of the most obvious differences? Why do you think such changes were made?*

- *Recall some of your own story of being catechized—some of its most obvious features, memorable stories, interesting aspects? What wisdom do you draw from these memories now?*

7

|| • *How about your own story of being a catechist? How has*
|| *that developed and changed, remained the same? Why?*

One of the many privileges of old age is that while feeling in our bones the weight of the past, we also carry in our heart and our mind all its riches. And when we take a leisurely time to let our memories well up to consciousness, some wonderful things may happen. We often feel revitalized, filled with wonder and gratitude and also hope for the future.

For instance, when I look back on my long journey as a catechist I can still feel the enthusiasm with which my friends and I moved on from one catechetical discovery and adventure to another as the biblical, liturgical, theological and catechetical movements of this century were developing, before and after Vatican II, and it fills my heart with gratitude. How privileged we were indeed to live in Europe when many of the prophetic figures of these times were teaching, publishing their books or having them translated: Congar, Chenu, Rahner, Schillebeeckx, Häring, Teilhard de Chardin, Daniélou, de Lubac, Jungmann, to name only a few. How we devoured those books and discussed them eagerly!

It seems that having been so enriched by that long past journey helps us to see the present situation with more clarity and serenity. Indeed we discern more willingly how the Spirit gently leads us to progress through the ups and downs of the road. Strangely, it might also help us anticipate more boldly and confidently the changes that will have to occur in the future if we want to follow the lead of the Spirit and respond to the signs of the time.

I will try to summarize briefly that long journey in the light of the last article written by Johannes Hofinger and published after his death in the 1984 summer issue of *The Living Light,* "Looking Backward and Forward: Journey of Catechesis" (vol. 20, n. 4). Perhaps because it was summertime this article did not get the attention it deserved. Indeed, what it called for in its conclusion, without spelling it out, was a pastoral and spiritual renewal in catechesis—

exactly what we are trying to make happen today. On the tenth anniversary of his death, this chapter is written in special homage to this great pioneer catechist of our time.

When I started my own initiation journey in Europe, the catechetical scene was still pretty much dominated by different types of "Baltimore Catechisms." They were made up of questions and answers and a few brief explanations. There were at least three sizes of print. In Grade One we began learning the material in the largest print, and the older we grew the more fine print we had to learn. By the end of elementary school we knew the whole book by heart. I was raised in France until I was ten years old. Then I was sent to boarding school in England for five years, so I had to learn my catechism in two languages!

However, when I was growing up, the first phase of the modern catechetical renewal was underway. The catechist was not only a repetitor as was the case during Father Hofinger's childhood, but was gradually being trained to become a pedagogue. That first phase of the modern catechetical movement started in central Europe with the search for a *better method.* Otto Willmann, a leading Catholic pedagogue of that time, helped catechists open up to new educational principles: presentation, explanation and application became the three main steps of good teaching. Later on in this country, Dewey's ideas also helped catechists move on to a more active method, involving the students in different ways and thus stimulating their interest. The catechist had really become a *teacher.* During those years, in the 1920s and 1930s, the biblical and liturgical renewals were getting underway and attracting more and more open-minded Catholics. Thus it prepared the way for a second phase in the catechetical movement which would be called the *kerygmatic renewal.*

The Austrian Jesuit Joseph Jungmann was the pioneer and main artisan of this renewal. But when in 1936 he published his remarkable book *Die Frohbotschaft und unsere Glaubensverkundigung (The Good News and Our Proclamation of Faith)* the Church was not ready for it, and it had to be withdrawn from the market. It took twenty-three years for the book to be published in English, with many cautious notes added.[1]

Tremendous progress was made possible thanks to this kerygmatic approach. For some time the existentialist philosophers had been drawing attention to the importance of personal spiritual experience and conviction with regard to religious faith. Building on that new awareness Jungmann invited the catechists to become the *heralds* (*keryx*) of the Good News whose power they would have personally experienced. They were also invited to concentrate on the core of the Christian message, the kerygma, which is the Good News of God's redeeming love manifested in the life, death and resurrection of Christ. That *evangelization*, proclamation of the Good News, was aimed at awakening in the students a loving response to God's love and to God's call to live by Christian values. Finally, it was hoped, this loving response would allow a progressive maturation of the faith. It was also the time when we were discovering the importance of what we then called Salvation History, and I can still see the great panels we would build illustrating the Creation, the Fall, the Paschal Mystery, the beginning of the Church and the Eschatological Kingdom. And what beautiful celebrations we would build around those themes! We really believed "that was it"!

For sure, Jungmann's influence was decisive. All Roman and National Directories around the world are still reaffirming Jungmann's basic insights. However, as always when we focus our attention mainly on one aspect of reality, we risk losing sight of another one. In our enthusiasm for the simple life-giving message we were trying to transmit, we did not pay enough attention to the recipient of the message. God's Word is always addressed to individuals or groups who are at a particular stage of development and live in a particular historic, cultural and social environment. Thus, after having focused our attention on the *method*, then on the *con-*

tent of catechesis, we began focusing it on the *recipient:* children and adolescents. So in the mid-1960s, the time was ripe for a new phase in the catechetical renewal.

That third phase was called the *human* or *anthropological* or *experiential approach*. We began to listen more to what the social sciences had to say to us: psychology, anthropology, sociology, etc. We became aware of many new dimensions of our task and mission: the need to start with the human experiences of the catechized, to be more attentive to the child's psychological development and to the cultural background of people. We began looking at our teaching more like a sharing, a facilitating process; especially in dealing with adults we realized the need for pre-evangelization. Liberation theology helped us in many ways. Under its influence we became more vividly aware of the crucial role of the community of faith, of the need for critical reflection and of the importance we should give in religious education to the commitment to justice, to peace and to the preference for the poor.

In the last ten years the RCIA has helped us understand more and more the need for adult education and the importance of the sponsoring role of the community and of liturgical experience in the growth and maturation of faith. Two major documents played a decisive role in this third phase of the catechetical movement: the General Catechetical Directory published in 1971 and our National Catechetical Directory which was published in 1977. It had been prepared by an extensive nationwide consultation which made people feel part of the process. This is probably why it was so well received and played such an important and creative role in shaping religious education in the following years.

This brings us to the present time and to this fourth phase which Father Hofinger proposed to call a pastoral phase. Before describing what he meant, let us see briefly what evaluation he proposed of the third phase. In spite of tremendous progress in many areas, notably in the quality of our curricula and the formation and dedication of the catechists, Father Hofinger wrote: "We are forced to admit that the final result of our educational efforts is, not just once and again, but very often, disappointingly unsatisfactory. We simply cannot deny that to a high percentage of our students God and Christ mean very little at the end of their juvenile religious instruction. All too many of them have not come to a religious commitment of any depth and lasting results in their lives . . . and end up in a thoroughly secularized style of life. The most significant and alarming fact seems to be the following: over the whole country we find countless cases in which young people who are hungry for more personal contact with God leave our Catholic community and try to find religious experience and true brotherhood in other groups." This judgment may seem quite severe but I think most of us would agree that he was right.

As we all know, many different socio-cultural factors were responsible for the situation, aside from our own failures as a Christian community. What Father Hofinger proposed to recover from those ailments was a pastoral approach to religious education. He rightly said that all the very positive acquisitions and fruits of the third phase should be kept alive but that we should now move on to a fourth phase. The main thrusts of what he suggests might be described as follows:

— Priority should be given to the religious and moral values throughout the whole process of religious education.
— Ongoing spiritual care should be provided to all educators, parents and teachers.
— This would only be achieved if there was a general religious renewal in our parishes, which requires more pastoral integration of everything related to religious education.

Even if they are not expressed with the "in" words of today, these thoughts are the very precious and truly prophetic legacy which Father Hofinger has left us. He was a very humble man, and it pleases me to pay tribute to him in trying to explicate in my own way the intuitions he did not have time to develop for us in detail. This is what I will attempt to do in the following chapters.

Appropriation to Life

- *What helpful insight have you gleaned from this historical overview for your present pastoral situation?*

- *Is there a decision or commitment that this review of catechetical history invites from you? What is it? What would it mean for your own ministry of catechesis?*

Chapter Two

An Important Paradigmatic Shift

Focus for Reflection

As the Bible says, "Without the vision, the people perish" (Prov 29:18). How true this is! To lose our sense of purpose is to become lifeless.

The best hopes we have—our vision—are so significant for any function of ministry, indeed for our whole life. What we most desire and aspire to gives a very definite "spin," a style and élan, to everything we do. Lack of a sense of noble purpose likely has equally deleterious consequences!

* *Pause and take a "blue sky" time about your own ministry. What is the vision that motivates it—the best hopes you have for it? Don't be reluctant to "dream the dream"!*

* *Continuing to "blue sky" it. How would you describe the "ideal" catechetical situation, including some of its most salient features?*

* *From where do you get such dreams and plans?*

Paradigm is one of those "in" words which many people use to describe different things. The simplest definition of it I found was in the Newsletter edited by Robert Humphrey: "Paradigms are the lens through which we view the world. They are the mental framework we impose on our perceptions in order to give them coherence and make sense of them."[1] Paradigms affect both our vision of reality and our actions. In the catechetical journey of this century which I just described, there were many paradigmatic shifts. Over the years our vision changed through a critical evaluation of the situation, and that vision led to a change in the course of action. A paradigmatic shift almost always meets with resistance at first (and sometimes for a long period) from those who either do not see the need for it or who benefit from the status quo.

As I said in the Introduction I believe we are experiencing today a major paradigmatic shift in our vision of and approach to religious education. That shift has been brought about, it seems to me, by three major factors:

1. A more vivid awareness of the socio-cultural changes that have been occurring in the world at large and in our North American society in particular.

2. A new willingness and courage to look at the pastoral and educational scenes with more realism, with a more critical eye and with greater honesty. We are willing, in the words of Father Patrick Brennan, to break up our addiction to things that don't work anymore.

3. An amazingly rich production of theoretical reflection and of pastoral and educational experiences which, having become widely known through books, magazines, conventions, networks and newsletters, have in turn created many new trends.

For the past thirty years I have been amazed by the quality of many of the theoretical catechetical publications in this country. I believe they are among the richest and most diversified in the world. It is impossible to cite all the authors, books, magazines and articles that deserve acknowledgment. However I wish to mention one recent book which has had an international impact and which brings together many of the trends of the past fifteen years or so. Thomas Groome's *Sharing Faith* (Harper Collins, 1991) might well be one of the books which can help us move on to the next phase on our catechetical journey. I believe the first part of the book, "Foundations," is one of the most comprehensive philosophical/theological reflections on the nature of religious education that is currently available. I hope writers and editors of curriculum materials in the coming years will take the time and trouble to study it and discuss it thoroughly before beginning their work. It is in my opinion a foundational theoretical text with regard to the holistic vision of religious education toward which we have been moving during recent years. About the rest of the book which describes the Shared Christian Praxis Approach and its various applications, I will offer some comments later on in Chapter Six which deals with religious literacy and curriculum design.

Among the major trends which have been and are shaping the paradigmatic shift we are experiencing, I would like to mention eight because of their direct impact on religious education:

- family consciousness
- small communities
- parish renewal with its emphasis on evangelization
- the RCIA with its latest offspring of Lectionary catechesis
- early childhood education
- intergenerational catechesis
- ongoing adult education
- the thirst for spirituality

The main ideas I will discuss either to affirm them or to critique them are somewhat connected to those major trends. I will focus on four major topics:

- the need to clarify and affirm the paradigmatic shift in our vision of and approach to religious education;

- the theological vision, the dominant image which might inspire and shape our search for progress and excellence in religious education;
- the structural changes that seem to be needed if we are to move toward that vision and to implement that approach;
- some of the practical consequences of that shift in our vision and our approach on certain key aspects of religious education, such as the overall design of the religious education journey, the concern for religious literacy and religious practice, and the thrust toward early childhood education.

A major paradigmatic shift always creates in its beginnings a somewhat confusing situation. This is normal. But it is then important to clarify its components so we can see where we want to go, where we don't want to go, and how we want to allow that shift to deploy its potential. The two main characteristics of the shift we are experiencing can be described, it seems to me, as a move toward a more holistic vision of religious education and a more pastoral approach to it.

Before explicating what I mean by these two terms and by the perspectives of renewal they open up for us, let me state something: I believe the seeds for many of the perspectives I will share with you were already present in some of the most important catechetical documents which haved shaped our efforts during the last decade—in particular, the National Catechetical Directory. But these perspectives were more implicit than explicit, and they remained somewhat ineffective for two reasons:

— our awareness of the socio-cultural changes was much less vivid and accurate than it is today;
— we were dominated by the school model and instructional aspects of religious education.

As a result, our major concerns centered around better curriculums, and we experienced the golden age of publishing. New series were constantly coming out and teacher training workshops were covering the country. This development brought about great progress in the quality of our curriculums, but perhaps it also blocked our view of fundamental problems, such as those we are facing today. Let me now explain what I mean by a holistic vision of and a pastoral approach to religious education.

1. Holistic Vision

I think it fair to say that in the past our practice, if not our theory or vision of our task in religious education, was somewhat dominated by our concern for *instruction* and *sacramentalization.* We are now moving toward a more holistic view, which different authors seek to describe in various ways. They talk about:

• facilitating ongoing conversion and moving toward discipleship;
• reaching down to the core of the being;
• teaching for the heart, mind and soul;
• educating for wisdom;
• facilitating belonging and not only believing;
• educating for personal and social transformation.

Pope John Paul himself has been calling for such a move since 1979 when he wrote: "Catechesis needs to be continually renewed by a certain broadening of its concept, by the revision of its methods, by the search for suitable language, and by the utilization of new means of transmitting the message" (*Catechesis in Our Time,* #17). All these expressions emphasize differently that in religious education we should be aiming with vivid awareness at a more global, comprehensive, holistic achievement—one that can only be attained and deployed over a lifetime and within the realm of a truly nurturing Christian community.

2. Pastoral Approach

As our vision of religious education becomes more holistic, our approach to it becomes more pastoral. We realize increasingly that our efforts on behalf of religious education should be less fragmented, more global, more coordinated and comprehensive; they should bring about more cooperation, more sharing of ideas, responsibilities and resources on the diocesan and parish levels.

Let me explain what I mean, limiting myself for the moment to the parish level. Perhaps the best words to characterize the pastoral approach I am advocating are *integration* and *cooperation*. In this approach the primary educator is or should be the parish community. The whole community is responsible for the transmission of the Christian tradition to the next generation, not just a few dedicated catechists or teachers. This is what I mean by an approach that stresses integration and cooperation.

This type of approach operates on two levels: structural and educational.

1. On a *structural level*, a pastoral approach fosters ongoing, organic, dynamic cooperation between the following sectors or ministries in parish life: evangelization, Christian initiation (that is, RCIA, RCIC), religious education, sacramental preparation, liturgical life, youth ministry, family life, young adult ministry, ongoing adult education, and all caring and healing ministries. This enumeration itself brings out the greatest challenge we face today, namely, that true renewal of religious education cannot happen without a general parish renewal.

2. On an *educational level*, a holistic vision of and integrative approach to religious education requires and makes possible ongoing, practical interaction of different realities, for example:

• spiritual experience and formation, both individual and communal;

- regular formal teaching during the school year for children and teenagers;
- quality liturgical experiences for everyone;
- effective apprenticeship in the Christian way of life for children and youth, both in daily family life and in the community through participation in the caring activities of the parish or neighborhood;
- a variety of ongoing educational opportunities for all adults, especially young adults and parents.

A cooperative and integrative approach is possible only if the pastoral staff and the parishioners engaged in parish or school ministries share a common vision of Catholic identity and the mission of the Church and feel collectively responsible for the Christian initiation of new generations.[2] For this dream to come true, we need to redirect our imagination and our educational creativity.

Our creativity during the past twenty-five years or so was geared mainly toward finding new pedagogies, more creative activities, and more fruitful dialogues, and developing better curriculums. These efforts, of course, should continue. But it seems to me that our creativity and imagination should now be directed more precisely toward pastoral concerns. These concerns might be expressed in a foundational question like the following:

How can we provide a diversified, flexible and ongoing support system for the development of a quality Christian life in the young of our communities, in their families and in the adult population?

Because of the very nature of Christian life, this continuing support system and quality development require three main ingredients:

— a truly personalized educational care for each child and adolescent through a variety of small groups concerned with cate-

chesis, spiritual life, and apprenticeship in Christian life (only the small groups allow for the personal mentoring which is needed);
— a much closer, personalized, diversified and lasting cooperation with the families of these youngsters;
— a more efficient support network made up of meaningful, personal inter-generational relationships and of a variety of small intentional communities within the larger community.

These ingredients would provide the diversified, flexible and ongoing support that children, teenagers, young adults and parents need if they are to lead a truly Christian life in our society today.

Appropriation to Life

• *How does Francoise's "vision" enrich your own? How would yours add to her proposal?*

• *Think of one realistic strategy that you can take on to enhance your parish, school, or family as "a nurturing Christian community." How will you try to implement it?*

Chapter Three

The Theological Foundation of the New Approach

Focus for Reflection

The word "symbol" comes from the Greek term symbole *meaning "to draw things together." Symbols help us to gather up a lot of different pieces and draw them together into one compelling expression. The social scientists also tell us that a good motivating symbol can have a powerful influence on our work, on our lives, on our very identity; our symbols shape what we do and who we are. For example, just seeing the five interlocked rings of the Olympic logo can be a powerful motivation for the aspiring young athlete, or the Hippocratic oath can remind a doctor of the very meaning of her/his profession.*

- *Choose a motivating symbol that helps you to "gather up," express, and renew your best hopes for your ministry of catechesis (this can be a word, statement, thing, gesture—any mode of expression).*

- *What are some of the sources of your symbol—influences, experiences, memories, reasons, and so on?*

- *What are some of its implications, its invitations, for you personally? For your catechesis?*

Any deep, lasting structural and pastoral move or change of direction must be rooted in a theological foundation inspired by a dominant image. I submit to you that the dominant image, which can inspire and shape our holistic vision of and pastoral approach to religious education, is the mysterious and over-arching symbolic reality of the Kingdom or Reign of God. Becoming more vividly aware of the Reign of God as the "metapurpose" of religious education, as Tom Groome puts it, is a basic prerequisite, it seems to me, in our move toward a new approach in religious education.

There are of course many different interpretations of this very rich and multifaceted symbolic reality. The way I will attempt to describe it here to enlighten our educational purpose is based principally on the insights of one of the greatest theologians of this century, Edward Schillebeeckx.

Following his two great books describing his christology: *Jesus, An Experiment in Christology* and *Christ, The Experience of Jesus as Lord,* published in the Netherlands in 1974 and 1977, he had planned to write a treatise on ecclesiology. But, as he explains in the Foreword of this last book, he changed his mind because he was deeply disappointed that the profound changes in the Church's self-understanding which Vatican II called for were finally minimized by the Vatican's bureaucracy.[1] So he decided instead to write a book which would summarize what he calls "the liberating theology I tried to draw out of the great Christian Tradition."[2] This marvelous book is written in a much simpler language and clearer style than his previous ones, and Schillebeeckx's hope is that what he offers us in this book will help us to "penetrate in the heart of the Gospel and of our Christian faith."[3] Indeed it does. In a pivotal chapter, dealing with the mystery of Jesus, he stresses that the Kingdom or Reign of God is a key word in Jesus' message. It expresses, he writes, "the biblical way of describing the divine essence: unconditional and liberating love. . . ."[4]

Out of the rich analysis he then proposes let me emphasize

three major points which are the basis of the description I will offer as the theological foundation of our holistic vision of religious education.

- "The Kingdom of God is the very presence of God among men, a presence which is active, stimulating and salvific inasmuch as it is welcomed and accepted."[5]
- That loving presence is freely offered to all but must also be freely accepted if it is to bear its fruit. When it is thus accepted it brings about a change of heart, a "metanoia" which profoundly transforms human beings' relationships with God and among themselves.
- "The Kingdom of God is essentially related to the person of Jesus."[6] Indeed, it is only through the life and teachings of Jesus that we can truly understand both what the gift of God's loving presence can mean and what liberating and transforming effect it can have on our life, on our societies and on our relationship with all of creation.

Building on these powerful insights I will now attempt to explicate them in a way which might enlighten the holistic approach our educational ministry is moving into.

The Reign of God then has to do first of all with God's self-revelation in the Jesus-event and in the Jesus-way. In Jesus, God discloses to us the wonder-filled mystery of the divine nature as a community of persons and a mystery of communion.

We find in the Bible two names of God which seem to give us a glimpse into the nature of God. The first one is in the Hebrew Scriptures in Exodus 3:13–14. Moses, who is afraid to go to his people with God's message, says to God, *"If they ask me, Who is sending you? What is His Name? What will I tell them?"* God answers: *"You will tell them, **I am** [Ego eimi] sent me to you."* For us, of course, this name evokes the idea of Being, of Life, of Source and Origin, of God as Ground of our Being. But it remains obscure and quite metaphysical.

The other name is given to us in the Christian Scriptures. John, summing up his experience of Jesus and of the Reign of God, writes: *"My beloved, love one another because God is love. Whoever does not love cannot know God. But whoever loves is born of God, and knows God, for God is love"* (1 Jn 4:7). Does not this second name explicate for us the true meaning of the first one, *Ego eimi,* as it was reflected and manifested through the person and life of Jesus? Indeed, we needed the Word Made Flesh to give to *Ego eimi* its true meaning in human terms. Through that revelation in Jesus, we discover all at once who God is—Father/Mother, Son and Spirit, mystery of communion and relationships—and what the Reign of God is about.

In discovering who God is and what the Reign of God is about, we begin to understand who we are and what we are called to become. Indeed, through the life and teachings of Jesus, we discover that the Reign of God is about our being invited to:

- share in God's own life and happiness,
- become divinely human or humanly divine, in the manner of Jesus through the gift of the Spirit,
- discover God's loving presence at the very core of our being and in the dailiness of our lives,
- live in communion with one another so as to live in communion with the Trinitarian God,
- share in God's dream for humankind, which is to bring all of us to fullness of life into the community of love.

As Schillebeeckx strongly underlines, the Reign of God, if we look at it through the praxis of Jesus, is essentially a liberating, saving reality. How are we to understand that with regard to our educational and pastoral ministry? Mainly in three ways, it seems to me:

1. It is psychologically and spiritually liberating for each one of us. In revealing to us that we are unconditionally loved by a gracious God, not for what we do, but for who we are, it helps us overcome the existential anguish stemming from the awareness of the fragility of our life and of the insignificance of our individuality. Because we are so loved by God we are freed to love ourselves and to love others.

2. The Reign of God is also liberating and transforming for society itself because God's love restores every human being to his or her personal dignity. One of the most striking things about Jesus' praxis in the Gospels is his attitude toward all those who are, in one way or the other, marginalized and despised or simply ignored by society: the poor, the sick and disabled, the sinners, the ignorant, the "politically incorrect," even women and children who were often, as both Schillebeeckx and Marcus Borg point out, considered as "nobodies."[7] Not only does Jesus respect all these people, but he defends them, heals them, describes them as privileged guests of the Kingdom and shares meals with them, which in his society, as Borg notes, was an extremely significant and politically explosive gesture.[8]

When people are thus restored in their sense of dignity, they are not magically freed from their problems and the oppression they endure, but they are ready to stand up for their ideas and their rights, and to seek for themselves and others that same dignity, that fullness of life for all which the Kingdom of God is about. So the Reign of God is also about reaching out to other people to feed if they are hungry, to find them if they are lost, to heal them if they are sick, to free them if they are victimized, to bring them together if they are alienated. And it is also about celebrating the joy of the Covenant which is offered to them all. This Reign of God is all at once a gift of love, a way of life, a fellowship and a community open to all. It is already there and forever coming. And, as many liberation theologians point out, these "privileged guests" are the ones who know best how to celebrate festively together the joy of the King-dom which is theirs![9]

3. Finally, the Reign of God, as we look at it through the prax-is of Jesus, is also liberating religiously. Indeed, Jesus repeatedly challenges those who abuse the spiritual power they claim for themselves and who burden the people with the doctrinal and rit-ual intricacies of the Law; he constantly brings them back to the unique commandment of love, to the necessity of faith and trust in God's love.

How important it is that we keep all those insights in mind when we carry out our ministry in religious education. If the Reign of God and the praxis of Jesus truly inspire our ministry we will always remember that religious education, for whatever age level, is not about indoctrinating and controlling people, it is about freeing them from their fears and alienations and facilitating their personal encounter with God so they can live to the full in the lib-erating joy of the Kingdom.[10]

In welcoming and experiencing the Reign of God, we discover an amazing and fundamental reality: the Reign of God is an un-conditional gift, a gift without strings, a gift offered to all. There are no prerequisites or requirements, except one: that we receive it with an open heart as a child receives a gift of love (Mk 10:25). This is what it means when we say that God is pure love.

There is however a radical risk, or rather two risks. The first one is that if we truly open our heart to that gift which is loving communion with God, with others and with all of creation, and taste its pure, divine joy even once, we will never be satisfied with any-thing else. We will spend the rest of our lives searching for that joy. The second risk is that once we have opened our heart to the inti-mate call we hear in the Kingdom to share the gifts of love, hope and joy, we will never again find peace if we turn away from it. If this is so, we might wonder why so many of our young people are leaving the Church today, looking elsewhere to quench their spiritual thirst.

Would it be because they had never truly discovered, experienced and tasted the reality and the joy of the Reign of God, of the liberating and loving Presence of God, in the first place? Or could it be that having experienced and tasted it in their own way, at the core of the raw stuff of their life—of their fears and their dreams, of their struggles, joys and longings (because this is where the Spirit is present and where she is active)—they were never able to link that experience with the abstract, sometimes alienating world of their religious knowledge? Could it be that the way we teach religion might sometimes block the revelation of the Reign of God at the core of their being and at the heart of their life? Could it be that we have been so busy with the Church, its doctrines, laws and rituals, that we have forgotten about the Reign of God? Or worse, could it be that we have confused and identified the Church and the Kingdom? Have we forgotten that the Church is not an end but a means, that the Church was created to usher in the Reign of God, that the Church is the Servant and the Reign of God is the goal?

Rediscovering that the Kingdom, the Reign of God, is at the heart of our faith and our ministry would bring us, I believe, to the spiritual conversion we need to move to a more holistic vision of and a pastoral approach to religious education. This rediscovery would also help us in two other ways. First, it would help put the legitimate concern for religious literacy in its rightful place. I believe the lack of understanding and experience of the Kingdom is a more important factor than is religious illiteracy in the alienation of the young from the Church. But I also believe that religious literacy is very important—in its proper time and place. Second, a rediscovery of the Reign of God at the heart of our life and ministry would help us find the proper perspective we should give to religious practice. It is also, of course, a legitimate concern—but in its proper time and place. I shall return to these two "hot points" later on.

Appropriation to Life

- *How do you respond to Francoise's proposal of "the Reign of God" as a symbol for the overarching vision of cate-chesis? Are there some assets? Some liabilities?*

- *Look again at your own sense of purpose as a catechist. Is there anything you want to reemphasize, renew or adjust?*

PART TWO

PRACTICAL
APPLICATIONS

❖

Chapter Four

The Need for Structural Changes

Focus for Reflection

Chapter 9 of St. Luke's Gospel recounts the commissioning and sending forth of "the Twelve" (Lk 9:1–6). Then, in chapter 10 we read: "After this, the Lord appointed seventy others, and sent them out two by two. . . ." (See Lk 10:1–12)

"Others" refers to people from the general group of disciples. On examining the two texts, note that the mission given to both groups is basically identical:
- *to preach the reign of God,*
- *to heal human brokenness,*
- *to engage with and depend on the community.*

At bedrock, all Christians are to participate in the common ministry of Jesus Christ.

- *Now, think about it! Why do you think Jesus sent them out "two by two"? What did this mean for their ministry?*

- *With whom are you called into partnership in your own ministry?*

- *What are some of the conditions needed for real cooperation within the life of a parish?*

33

As was suggested in Chapter Two, a pastoral approach to religious education would require ongoing, organic, dynamic cooperation between all sectors of parish life. Therefore on a structural level, the basic, concrete challenge we face in trying to implement a cooperative and integrating approach is this: How can we respect the specificity, goals, methods and charisms of each ministry, agency, movement, etc., and get those involved to cooperate to avoid detrimental duplication, unnecessary competition, waste of energy, time, personnel, and money? How can we avoid having people fall between the cracks? How can we coordinate the efforts of all for the benefit of all? It seems to me that we cannot meet this challenge without some modifications in the way our structures usually function, both on a *parish level* and on a *diocesan level*. What might be those modifications? I will suggest two, but before describing them, let us briefly reflect on the drawbacks of the lack of cooperation on the parish level and on the major obstacles to that cooperation.

Both the drawbacks and the obstacles have been pointedly described by Richard Reichert in the excellent article I mentioned in Chapter Two.[1] One of the great obstacles to the cooperative involvement of the whole parish in religious education has been, paradoxically, the very zeal and generosity of the catechists themselves.[2] When *To Teach as Jesus Did* proposed the key words *message, community* and *service* as the guiding light of catechetics, Reichert argues that catechists "mistakenly concluded" that it was their responsibility to provide not only the teaching, but all the rest, namely "those lived experiences of welcoming, of fellowship, affective support and affirmation, prayer, worship, mission and service to others that in reality can only be provided by the family and the parish faith community." And he adds: "Just as tragic, we also convinced parents and parish that we both should and could do this."[3]

This misguided generosity of course led to burnout and discouragement for many catechists and passivity for the two other parties, the family and the parish. For a number of years now we have been trying to move out of this vicious circle, but it is not easy.

Another problem is what we might call a "compartmentalized mentality" about parish ministry. Each agency, structure, group, movement, tends to function in isolation from the others or with a minimum of cooperation, and it is very difficult to overcome this attitude. We all have had many experiences with this kind of mentality. Let me briefly review a few.

Reichert mentions the "competition that exists in many parishes between support for Catholic Schools and a commitment to quality parish religious education programs."[4] Even if great progress has been accomplished in the past few years, both catechists and children often feel like "second class citizens" in the parish. I heard about a group of CCD children who asked why the Catholic School children were always in the first rows of pews in church on First Communion day. They were told it was because they were better behaved and better rehearsed! But more detrimental is the fact that often those children are taught in huge numbers once a week, that catechists have no real possibility of cooperation with the parents, and that once the children are "sacramentalized" there is no follow-up, because of the lack of personnel and resources. How often was I saddened in the past while visiting diocesan offices of religious education to witness the lack of cooperation and sometimes the animosity between the two branches of education. But I am happy to say that in recent years I have sensed real progress in many dioceses, especially smaller ones.

However, this compartmentalized and competitive mentality is often found throughout the life of the parish. I remember spending a week in a large diocese, having been asked to go each evening to a different parish to speak to parents about the spiritual and moral development of the child. One parish had invited all parents from the Catholic School and the Parish Programs, and even invited neighboring parishes to join. But in the other parishes it was either Catholic School or Parish Program audiences. In one of them the principal came to me to say how much she regretted that she had not been notified. In another one a former student of mine in charge of family life complained that she had only learned that I was coming the week before, through the parish bulletin, after she had invited another speaker to present the same topic for another date!

Many more examples could be given of this lack of cooperation and its detrimental effects, but let us turn now to what seems to be in Reichert's mind another major cause of religious education's problems. It is what he calls "ecclesiological schizophrenia,"[5] whereby catechists often function with a Vatican II idea of the Church and of Christian education whereas the pastors and parish staffs often function in a pre-Vatican II mode. This of course creates a fundamentally dysfunctional situation with very negative consequences both for the catechists on a personal level and for their ministry.

So what can we do about that situation? I would like to propose two modifications in the way we usually function. The first modification has been described by Father Brennan in his wonderful book *Re-imagining the Parish.*[6] He suggests that all the "structures charged with coordination, facilitation and animation envision themselves as *communities* and act as such."[7] This means that their members must take the time to share Word, life and prayer as well as carry out their responsibilities. So, he says, instead of boards, councils and teams, we would have the religious education *community,* the worship *community,* the youth ministry *community,* the finance and administration *community,* etc. And "the parish governance bodies or parish councils could (also) be re-imagined as parish-leadership communities."[8] This, he believes, would powerfully contribute to transform the parish.

But this change in vision and praxis requires a true conversion in the parish leadership. It requires that the members of the boards, councils and teams responsible for the various ministries recognize the need to sit down together to share their vision of the Church, of Christian life and of ministry, and to move toward a common vision in the light of the Reign of God as the metapurpose and "raison d'être" of each of their ministries and of the parish itself. As the saying goes, "As we *see* Church so we *do* Church." It seems to me that one way of moving toward this "conversion" would be for those parish staffs to do some shared praxis with the help of books or articles which encourage them to open their hearts and minds to a more progressive and dynamic vision. Books like Brennan's *Re-imagining the Parish* or Maria Harris' *Fashion Me a People,* or this little book and many other books and articles could be read by different members and then discussed together leisurely. This first experience in sharing questions, problems and new ideas in a non-threatening atmosphere might help the participants gently move toward a more common vision and provide the incentive they need to gradually become ministerial communities.

The second modification has to do with long-term planning. To foster more cooperation, why not plan in two stages? First, the leadership communities of each ministry would meet to elaborate an initial stage of global, tentative planning. Then, at a general leadership meeting held under the inspiration of the Reign of God, dreams and concerns, ideas and plans would be shared, the allocation of resources discussed and plans eventually adjusted for better cooperation.

Why is this type of cooperation so difficult? What are we afraid of? Of losing power or prestige or money for our "little kingdom" as a school principal told me on one occasion? Or that our good ideas might be stolen? But isn't it the best thing that can happen to a good idea? And isn't the Reign of God more important than all our own little kingdoms?

The fruits of such a cooperative effort are obvious:

- Greater personal understanding and mutual appreciation and support instead of misunderstanding, rivalry or plain ignorance. The tensions are sometimes unbelievable!
- Greater appreciation of the goals of each ministry or group.
- The facility to smooth out problems that inevitably occur in day-to-day activities.
- The possibility of sharing creative ideas, solutions to problems, and eventually personnel and resources.
- The possibility of enhancing each other's activities through co-ordination.

The negative consequences of the lack of cooperation are also obvious and we all know what they are.

Moving on now to the diocesan level, it seems to me that one of the major tasks of the diocesan ministerial structures would be to encourage and facilitate that spirit of cooperation among the various diocesan boards, agencies and movements so that it can trickle down to the parish level. However it is probable that for this to happen diocesan structures would also need to go through the conversion process in the light of the Reign of God as the meta-purpose of their own level of ministry! Once that conversion is underway, why not plan a yearly three-day gathering for all diocesan ministries, agencies, movements, etc.?

Each ministerial community would come to such a gathering with a preliminary tentative plan of action. The first day would be spent sharing the Word, moments of prayer, of fellowship, and the tentative plans. The second day would allow for discussion to see how these plans might be coordinated whenever possible and adjusted so as to enhance cooperation and mutual support. The third day would allow time for each ministerial community to readjust their plan and would end with sharing of Word and prayer, and perhaps a celebration of the Eucharist and the renewal of everyone's commitment to work together as servants of the Reign of God. I am convinced that successfully attaining organic, dynamic and ongoing cooperation is one of the major components in our search for renewal and excellence in religious education.

Appropriation to Life

- *In your pastoral situation, how can you move toward greater cooperation? Among whom? Shared planning? How?*

- *What is your next step toward partnership and cooperation in your ministry? Will you take it?*

Chapter Five

A Theoretical Outline of the Overall Religious Education Journey

Focus for Reflection

The Bible often portrays the Israelites as a pilgrim people; the Second Vatican Council retrieved this image for the whole Church—a pilgrim people of God. Poets often image life itself as a journey that we travel; in a sense our whole life, including our faith, is the story of a "pilgrim's progress."

- *Drawing from your own life thus far, and from knowing well the lives of older Christians (grandparents, etc.), how would you describe the major milestones and turning points in the journey of Christian faith?*

- *What kind of catechesis do you think is needed in each phase of the journey? Why?*

Building on our new awareness of today's needs and on the positive aspects of today's trends—and having them interact—we can redesign perhaps more clearly the road map of the overall religious education journey. It is a *theoretical* guide because the children, adolescents and adults who come in touch with us at any given time are at different stages on the map. Also, even the best road map has to be adapted to the possibilities of the real people on the journey; people come first.

However, this outline is also *practical* because, as you will see, it is very concrete and specific in its suggestions. The overall journey, as we see it today, can be outlined in four stages; we will call them pre-evangelization,[1] evangelization, initiation, and ongoing adult education. As you see, I include under the title initiation (with regard to children and adolescents) the long road which begins with the awakening of faith and brings one to the threshold of adulthood. By then it might be assumed that the initiated have the capacity to make a mature decision about their commitment to a truly Christian way of life and to the sharing in the mission of the Church. This would mark the end of the initiation phase.

For each stage, I will try to do two things: first, describe what the journey is about, and, second, identify the different types of cooperative ministries which should be involved to bring out its full potential. Many of the statements in this description call for precisions or comments. These will be offered at the end of the chart; they will be announced by a number like [I].

1. Pre-Evangelization

What is it about?

- Pre-evangelization is about reaching out, creating bonds of friendship, entering each other's worlds. It is about discerning the cultural mythos of people, their dreams and fears, their felt needs, and the special richness or problems in their culture. It's about learning from them as well as sharing with them.
- Pre-evangelization is about trying to respond to people's needs by putting them in touch with one another, with parish or neighborhood organizations or groups. It's about cooperating in neigh-

borhood activities for justice, peace or mutual support. It's about revealing the good news of God's love, of God's reign, by our *deeds,* by the quality of our caring relationships.

What types of cooperative ministries are needed?

A "reach out" type of ministry for which any parishioners could qualify, provided they are persons of deep faith, aware of their responsibility in the mission of the Church, and gifted for interpersonal relationships.

What is the expected outcome of this pre-evangelization?

The expected outcome is, hopefully, awakening in some people the desire to know more about the Gospel that inspires our life and bringing them to face the fundamental questions of the meaning and purpose of their own life.

2. Evangelization

What is it about?

- Evangelization is about beginning to share the good news through our *words* as well as our deeds.
- It's about offering the opportunity to discover certain aspects of the community's life, for example, occasionally inviting someone to share in a Sunday liturgy, in a catechetical group or youth group, in a family life activity, in a Bible study group, or to participate in a community's special activity for social justice, political action, caring ministry, or just a fiesta.
- In simple, informal ways evangelization awakens one's awareness that the Reign of God is at hand and that God's loving presence is at the core of our life as a gift offered to all.

What types of ministries are needed?

The same type of persons as in the pre-evangelization stage who would work in conjunction with those in charge of evangelization. Together they would minister through kitchen table conversations, inter-generational relationships, and small intentional communities adapted to the cultural background of people.

What is the expected outcome of this second stage of evangelization?

The expected outcome is, hopefully, developing in some people the readiness for an initial step toward conversion, which is an explicit desire to be initiated, a free commitment to a regular catechetical experience. Everything on this journey is dependent upon the person's liberty, freedom, and desire. Only then can we ensure the quality of the religious education journey.

3. Initiation

This stage covers a large segment of the journey and includes different types of travelers. The following distributions will attempt to take this into account. All catechetical activities at this stage should be carried out under the coordinating ministry of the Director of Religious Education (D.R.E.).

A. Children, adolescents, adults
who are not baptized

What is it about?

Children, adolescents or adults who are not baptized are invited at this stage to formally start the RCIA or RCIC journey. It is important to offer different types of journeys. Some people will need more personal mentoring, others more community experience. Some will require more intellectually sophisticated instruction than others. Inculturation and adaptation are of primary importance.

What types of cooperative ministries are needed?

The cooperative ministries involved in this catechumenal journey are all those related to the RCIA and RCIC. These should, however, also work in cooperation with all other parish ministries, as is required for the other categories of people journeying in the initiation process.

B. CHILDREN WHO HAVE BEEN BAPTIZED AND WHOSE PARENTS HAVE BEEN EVANGELIZED

What is it about?	What types of cooperative ministries are needed?
a) It is first about religious awakening in the home. To do this well, parents need practical help and encouragement.	Parents with the help of family life organizations: Marriage Encounter, Christian Parenting, etc.
b) Pre-school programs are desirable, not as a substitute but, hopefully, as a complement to the religious awakening happening in the home.	Pre-school teachers and catechists in cooperation with the parents.

What is it about?	**What types of cooperative ministries are needed?**
c) Regular catechesis during the school year in different settings and in small groups allowing for the personal spiritual care which is an essential element of the journey.	The parish catechists and Catholic school teachers with the help of parishioners either regularly or occasionally for special activities.
d) Meaningful Sunday Eucharist where special care is taken to facilitate children's active participation or where special Liturgies of the Word are offered.	The parish priests and liturgical teams, in cooperation with the parents and catechists.
e) Ongoing apprenticeship in the Christian way of life at home, such as habits of prayer and education to Christian values.	This belongs first of all to the parents, but once again with the cooperation of all those support groups in the parish who are concerned with helping families.
f) The apprenticeship of Christian values should also happen in the Catholic school and parish school of religion.	Parish catechists and all Catholic school personnel from the Principal to the teachers, to the secretaries, etc.

What is it about?	What types of cooperative ministries are needed?
g) The journey should also include regular participation in the caring ministries of the community, adapted to age, charisms, personal readiness and circumstances [I].	Parishioners who are involved in those ministries, who agree to sponsor one child or a small group of children in coordination with the parents and catechists.
h) We also need an immediate spiritual preparation for Eucharist and Reconciliation. This should be done mainly in the home according to personal readiness, but it should also occur in the parish so that it includes a community experience.	The parents as much as possible, with support from the D.R.E. and the catechists, and from other parishioners who are committed to that special sponsoring ministry, which is limited in time and scope. Praying partners from the elderly could also cooperate.
i) After the celebration of the Eucharist begins the last stage of initiation: *mystagogical catechesis,* which is the enrichment and deepening of the sacramental experiences. This is done, as before, through regular catechesis, the Sunday Liturgy, and participation in the caring ministry of the community as ways to "live the Eucharist" which we celebrate.	Catechists, Catholic school teachers, liturgical teams, caring ministries personnel, family life movements, ongoing parental involvement mainly with regard to day-to-day apprenticeship of the Christian way of life.

What is it about?	**What types of cooperative ministries are needed?**
j) During the mystagogical years special care should be given to the development of a personal life of prayer. Special opportunities should be offered for taking part in days of recollection, or regular prayer groups, or celebrations of the Word, or popular devotions on different occasions. Students should be initiated to different ways of praying according to their desire and readiness.	Parents, catechists and school teachers should relentlessly do their part and provide a gentle personal spiritual care. They should also ask the cooperation of other parishioners whose special gifts would contribute to that ministry.

C. ADOLESCENTS

What is it about?	**What types of cooperative ministries are needed?**
When children reach adolescence, the mystagogical journey should be planned and carried out in close cooperation with youth ministry activities. In this regard, the following special concerns should be kept in mind:	More than ever before, close cooperation is needed between parents, catechists, teachers, youth ministers, and all those involved in the various parish ministries and activities, from the Liturgy to the social and political endeavors.

What is it about?	**What types of cooperative ministries are needed?**
• providing teens with diverse and flexible opportunities for small group experiences so they can find a "community of trust," as Joe Moore calls it;	
• giving them more choices and responsibility for their own education and for the ways they want to pursue religious literacy and to participate in the life of the community; [II]	
• providing them with opportunities to develop personal relationships with adults from the community who are available to walk with them as adult friends and to share their hobbies, skills, cultural interests, or to just talk or go out.	Adults from the community should be given the opportunity to meet with adolescents to initiate friendly relationships with them with no other specific purpose.

4. Ongoing Adult Education

Once the initiatory journey is complete, the mission of the Church to young adults is to provide them with ongoing, diversified and flexible opportunities to deepen their spiritual life, to enrich their religious literacy, and to sustain their commitments to the Reign of God. This should be done, however, with a vivid awareness of the great complexities of life for the young adults in our society. As Father John Kuzik so rightly points out in his talks and writings, these young adults are in a time of their lives when a whole host of new problems and challenges face them, and they need the help and support of a community which is flexible, respectful, and caring, but never coercive.

To better serve the diverse needs of this young generation, it would probably be more feasible to coordinate services available on a diocesan or regional basis rather than on a parish basis. I believe that the Chicago Young Adult Ministry Service is a wonderful example of what can be done along those lines in a large city. In rural areas a regional cooperation would be required.

Additional Comments Concerning the Religious Education Journey

It seems quite obvious that this road map is impossible to follow without the *conversion of the parish leadership* to a holistic vision of and a cooperative approach to religious education. Indeed, each one of these stages can only be experienced in its full richness if there is all along active cooperation of all the ministries we mentioned. The *whole community* must be constantly challenged to live up to its responsibility in sharing its faith and traditions with the new generations in a great variety of ways.

It is critical for the authenticity, the genuine quality of the journey, that all along the spiritual quest for God, the longing, the desire for communion with God be awakened and nourished. It is this desire that initiates and sustains the ongoing process of conversion, which is at the heart of the journey. This desire, of course, is mainly a gift of the Spirit. But our responsibility is to actively prepare the way for the Spirit's mysterious action and provide the means for enhancing it through quality spiritual experiences and meaningful personal spiritual care.

The passage from one stage to the other can never be automatic or mandatory; it is linked to personal readiness in the ongoing process of conversion, which is at the heart of the journey.

[I] Participation in the caring ministries of the community

I would like to insist on this aspect of the journey. Service is supposed to be part of the journey, and we teach about it. But teaching about it and doing it are two different things. If religious education is to be truly an initiation into a community, an apprenticeship in the Christian way of life, this aspect of the journey is very important. How can children and youth get a true image of what the Church is about, of what being a Christian is about, if they do not concretely see and take part in the caring ministry of the Church except for a few weeks during their Confirmation programs when the "obligation to serve" suddenly comes out of the blue? The invitation to serve should be adapted, of course, to age and possibilities. It should propose a variety of activities or relationships, but it should be ongoing.

One objection to our efforts to enlarge and enrich the total experience of holistic religious education is the lack of time, for parents as well as for children. On that question, I would like to endorse a comment made by Joe Moore in an excellent article in a recent issue of *The Living Light.*[2] He breaks up the *"myth of no time."* He believes, as I do, that when we offer people experiences that are truly meaningful, life-giving, and adapted to their felt needs, culture and degree of readiness, they find time to come and they enjoy them. Both children and adolescents often find great satisfaction and interest in simple experiences of sharing in the caring ministry of their community, provided we engage them in the right way. Let me quote Joe Moore from the same article: " . . . young hearts need experiences to move them to tenderness. Service projects in parish programs often fail in this regard. I think Gustavo Gutierrez hit the nail on the head when I heard him say that a well-off person can feel little for the poor and oppressed and not be moved to social justice unless he or she has at least one friend who is poor and oppressed. In other words, the key to caring about the world lies in our interpersonal relationships. We cannot be moved by statistics, abstract concepts, or emaciated faces on television. Not until we have a relationship with someone can we feel their pain. This is what we can do for young people: provide them with the opportunities to meet the disenfranchised. When they become a part of the life of the unshaven old man in the soup kitchen or the child in rags who pulls at their arm they will begin to understand exactly how much they can matter."[3]

But I also believe we should build upon the neighborhood gang phenomenon which bears witness to the tremendous capacity of young people for initiative and coordinated action. Why not encourage the teens to apply those dynamic energies to improving the quality of life in the neighborhood as part of the "service" dimension of their journey? This would be also an excellent opportunity to engage them in *shared Christian praxis* to help them reflect together on those experiences.

[II] What about confirmation?

You probably noticed that I did not mention Confirmation along this journey. Don't worry. I will not enter this explosive debate at length! I would just like to offer two or three brief remarks.

a) One remark concerns the way the Catechism of the Catholic Church approaches the Sacrament. It acknowledges that Confirmation is a sacrament of initiation, "perfecting the grace of Baptism." But it insists that those who receive it, and I quote, "are more strictly obliged, as true witnesses of Christ, to spread and defend the faith by word and by deed" (Art. 2:1285). This, of course, tends to reinforce the opinion of those who see Confirmation as most appropriately celebrated toward the end of adolescence, as a kind of rite of passage toward a more responsible life.

Maybe it would be helpful before deciding when we want to

celebrate Confirmation to explore and reflect on secular rites of passage the young people experience, and what they mean to them. This, of course, would be different according to their various cultures. Let me give you some examples which friends of mine recently brought to my attention. In certain Spanish-speaking cultures the "quinsiniera" is a very significant ritual marking the passage from childhood to youth for the young girl, and the first shaving of the young boy by his father also has a very significant meaning as a rite of passage. In a more Anglo-Saxon culture the preparation for and granting of a driver's license is a decisive rite of passage from dependence to more freedom and responsibility. It seems to me that it would be wise to bring the young people into our discussion of the right time for Confirmation and the type of preparation it would require, because they know quite well what a rite of passage is about.

   b) A second remark is that, whatever is decided for Confirmation in a parish or diocese, I believe the adolescent religious education journey should be *much more richly ritualized* than at present. Rituals are a very important way for us to symbolize, to appropriate the meaning of and celebrate the many transitions in our lives. Celebrating our birthdays, for example, is a basic ritual that allows us to appropriate and celebrate the passing of time. It is an exciting experience of growth in the beginning, and a more nostalgic one when we are over the hill; but it remains an important one.
   Adolescence is essentially a rapid, intense and multifaceted experience of change, growth and transition from childhood to adulthood. On a secular level, we know that adolescent gangs create many rituals of initiation of their own. I believe we should do the same for the religious education journey of teenagers. We should help them move through those stages of growth and crises in the light of the Paschal mystery, as it is expressed in the baptismal and

eucharistic rituals and symbols. There is an amazing correspondence between the adolescent journey and those symbols and rituals. We might create with them meaningful ways of celebrating ritually vital initiatory experiences and themes, such as: from darkness to light, from fear to trust, from alienation to fellowship, from feeling lost to finding a home, from dependence to responsibility, from slavery to freedom, from confusion of identity to being called by name, from hatred of self and others to acceptance and love of self and others, from guilt to peace, from despair to hope, from death to life.

I am convinced that adolescents would have wonderful ideas in cooperation with us. I have heard of marvelous things happening with groups of adolescents who create their own rituals and initiate the younger ones who join their groups so they can grow in faith together. Let's use our imagination! These rituals, of course, should never be imposed at definite times by the catechists. Rather, they should grow out of the journey itself, determined by the readiness of each adolescent. Some would be celebrated within the age group, others with the parents, others with the community.

Toward the end of high school, this ritually rich journey might lead, for those who wish, to a special solemn, personal renewal of baptismal vows at the Paschal Vigil, adapted for this purpose; this would mark the end of the initiatory journey.

Community members would be challenged, as part of their own renewal of baptismal vows, to commit themselves to help and support this new generation in living its faith, but also to make room for it to take on right away its share of responsibility in the community. Some kind of pot-luck supper or social could be offered after the Vigil, bringing together the families of those young people and the community, especially all those who have cooperated in any way in their journey of faith over the years. It might be a wonderful way to foster a sense both of belonging and of responsibility in the adult community as well as in the young people.

Appropriation to Life

- As you review Francoise's proposal for the "overall journey" of Christian faith, what do you agree with? Disagree with? Do you have anything to add to her suggestions?

- What is the "next step" in your own faith journey? How will you take it?

Chapter Six

The Concern for Religious Literacy and Curriculum Design

Focus for Reflection

In his exchange with Pilate, John reports Jesus to say: "For this I was born and for this I came into the world, to testify to the truth. Everyone who belongs to the truth listens to my voice" (Jn 18:37). Jesus testifies on his own behalf that "the truth" was his life-purpose. Pilate, more as a throw-away dismissal rather than a real question, asks: "What is truth?" Jesus does not respond; he likely knew it would be a waste of time. But ever since then, his community of disciples, the Christian Church, has claimed to teach foundational "truths" of faith— for example, that God loves all humankind, and so on.

• *What are some of the core "truths" that constitute your own Christian faith?*

• *How and when would you want to teach these "truths" to others?*

• *What are your hopes for how other people might come to "know" the core truths of Christian faith? At what level of their being?*

1. Religious Literacy

For many years a great deal has been said and written about religious literacy. In some circles it has been and still is a dominant preoccupation, and the publication of the Catechism of the Catholic Church is considered to be *the* answer, *the* solution to address this concern. In other circles, however, the preoccupation for literacy seems irrelevant and outmoded. I would like to present here a middle-of-the-road view on the question.

I find it helpful to make a distinction between two types of literacy. The first is foundational and existential. It should be fostered from the beginning of life till the end. The second, cultural or theological, should be pursued with great discernment from around age ten or eleven right through adulthood. It is pursued more explicitly and boldly as the years go by.

A. Foundational/Existential Religious Literacy

Because the Reign of God is the metapurpose of religious education, foundational/existential religious literacy is inseparable from spiritual life, from meaningful liturgical experience and from personal moral experience.

Indeed, religious knowledge is not an end in itself. To be spiritually nourishing and life giving, it must be assimilated, that is, digested. As the Scandinavian philosopher, Søren Kierkegaard, wrote: "I only know a truth when it has become life in me." I was sixteen years old when I found that statement in Kierkegaard's *Treaty of Despair.* It has been my guiding light ever since.

The crucial question, then, if we want to achieve excellence in foundational religious literacy, is not, "How can we feed children all the doctrine in the Catechism of the Catholic Church before the end of high school?" Rather, it is, "How can we teach in a way that will awaken their appetite, their thirst for more religious knowledge as they grow up so that they are motivated to work for it over the years?" This, of course, will only happen if it has given them life, if it has enriched the meaning and purpose of their life at each stage of development.

Medicine tells us that appetite is very important to proper digestion and assimilation. The same is true on a spiritual level. While Jungmann's statement, "knowledge must furnish light for desire," remains true initially, it is my experience and belief that genuine spiritual experience—experience of the Reign of God—is what awakens the appetite, the desire, the longing for more religious knowledge. As Don Kimball said one day when we were discussing this point, "Who wants to learn more about somebody one has never met?"

When I was teaching at Fordham, we surveyed adolescents from a Catholic high school to find out who God was for them and what prayer meant to them after ten years of Catholic education. One of the boys gave an answer that has stayed with me until this day: "They have been talking to me about God for ten years but I don't know God. I have never met God, so why should I pray?" When the thirst is not there and spiritual experience is lacking, we merely indoctrinate; we do not nourish faith or foster foundational/existential religious literacy. The very practical question we therefore face is this: "How do we foster genuine, foundational religious literacy?" This, of course, is a very vast and complex question. The following reflections might shed some light on it and help initiate the research that seems to me urgent if we are to give it an adequate answer.

• We are beginning to see religious education as a lifelong process. If we really mean that, should we not take our time? Up to now it seems to me that we have interpreted this awareness as the need to prolong the duration of religious education for a lifetime. But we have not drawn its consequences with regard to the religious education of children and adolescents.

- Foundational religious literacy should not be measured by the *accumulation* of knowledge but by its *assimilation*. Truths have to become life.

Foundational religious literacy does not exist as a technical concept per se, like proper spelling, for instance. It is a holistic, developmental concept which should be described clearly and carefully for each stage of psychological development. The core of our faith is simple: it is the Good News of God's saving love manifested in the life, death and resurrection of Jesus, and in the gift of the Spirit. But the fullness of the Christian tradition developed over the centuries around this core is extremely rich and complex.

One of the basic questions we have to face then is not so much, "How can we break down the whole Corpus Doctrinae into small pieces, to present it a little at a time?" It is, rather, "How can we, over the years, enrich and complete the core of our faith by relating it constantly to the changing life experiences, questions, felt needs and longings of the growing child and adolescent today, in our society and in our different cultures?" We have, of course, already asked and answered that question. But I believe we did so taking theology into account much more than psychology and culture. We were guided, moreover, by an instructional model and an overwhelming concern for early sacramentalization more than by the holistic vision and perspective of ongoing adult education we have now.

This is why I believe that much more specific research is needed[1] to help us answer the following question: "Which elements of our traditions, of our Catholic doctrine, which stories, poems, parables and excerpts from our Scriptures, which symbols and rituals from our liturgy, which stories from the past history of the Church and from its present activities in the world, might be the most assimilable, the most meaningful, the most life-giving for each stage of psychological development in today's world, in today's different cultures?" We might discover with surprise that some things we had more or less left out, or passed over very superficially, might be very relevant today at a certain stage of development; I am thinking for instance of the doctrine about the Mystical Body and the Communion of Saints, while other things we had painstakingly tried to teach were irrelevant.

I am convinced that if we take seriously this question and act upon it, that is, teach children and adolescents in a way that is at once challenging, meaningful and life-giving for each stage of their development, they would return for more because they would have found meaning, purpose and stimulation for their life as it unfolded. I believe the real challenge of our search for excellence in foundational religious literacy is to give children and adolescents *all* they need, *only* what they need, and *when* they need it, so that the One Who is the Light and the Truth may become life in them.

This developmental approach does not mean that we "water down" either the doctrinal or the moral requirements of discipleship to what Father DiGiacomo calls "Brand X Religion." But it does mean that we present them in constant, meaningful and challenging correlation with the questions, felt needs and readiness of the growing child and adolescent. This requires that they must first be taken seriously and listened to rather than just talked to. Respecting children's needs and readiness does not mean that we wait passively for an interest to awaken, but that we create an environment and use a pedagogy which can stimulate more and new interests.

It also means that the more children grow up, the more we should be concerned not so much with, as Father William O'Malley writes, "dumping eminently forgettable data into their heads," as with teaching them how to think critically, how to reason, how to reflect, and pre-eminently how to read the Bible, how to understand it, interpret it, and meditate on it within our Catholic tradition. If we do that, they will be able to find in the Bible their inspiration to think, judge and decide for themselves over the years how to live their faith and bear witness to it. I would like to insist on this point for a moment because I believe it is of crucial importance. I will do it in the context of our next section.

B. *Cultural/Theological Religious Literacy*

We have talked about the importance of pursuing foundational/existential religious literacy because it is the basis for a quality Christian life. But it is also important, as the children grow through adolescence and adulthood, to pursue cultural, theological religious literacy. In today's pluralistic world, adolescents—and even children, especially at the end of elementary school—feel challenged in their Christian beliefs and values. So do many adults who have little formation. Catholic Christians need to feel competent and secure in their faith and self-identity if they are to be able to dialogue creatively with the secular culture, understand it, appreciate it, and challenge it when necessary. Our Christian way of thinking and of living is definitely counter-cultural in some ways, and we must help our youngsters understand why.

Our challenge is to make doctrinal formation intellectually meaningful and enriching so that youth and adults will be motivated to pursue it. But for that to happen the doctrine must be relevant. The intricacies and evolution of Catholic doctrine on minor points are not relevant for today's students. But the way we as Catholics theologically interpret the Bible, for instance, concerning creation, the resurrection, human rights, the dignity and equality of all people, and the preference for the poor, is extremely important. The doctrine of the Church on the struggle for justice and peace is eminently relevant and eminently part of our Catholic Christian identity—much more than the doctrine on indulgences. Let us, therefore, actively pursue theological literacy and foundational existential literacy in ways that are relevant to the questions people have to their degree of readiness and to the circumstances of our culture. Religious literacy as a means for a fuller Christian life is definitely part of our search for renewal and excellence in religious education. The following reflections will explicate what I mean by pursuing cultural/theological religious literacy.

a. The unique importance of biblical formation

Because of the overwhelming publicity given to the Catechism of the Catholic Church, another Roman publication has yet to receive the attention it deserves from religious educators; it is the last work of the Pontifical Biblical Commission: *The Interpretation of the Bible in the Church.*[2] The simultaneous publication of the two documents is indeed a blessing because the second one not only completes but corrects some of the shortcomings of the first one with regard to the use and interpretation of the Bible.[3]

As John Gillman points out in a brief but fascinating article on the history of the Pontifical Biblical Commission, its role can be a truly prophetic one because it is now composed not of cardinals named for life, but of twenty biblical scholars from around the world named for five years. Of course, "the ongoing question is how free the members of the Commission are to reach conclusions which may assist the Church's judgment to mature, even if possibly leading in a direction different than that envisioned by the Congregation of the Faith."[4]

Anyway this document is in my opinion an absolute "must" for all who are involved in religious education either in curriculum design or in teacher formation. Indeed, it seems to me that one of the great challenges we face as religious educators today with regard to the content of our faith is how to allow the Bible to become more and more what it is meant to be: ". . . the spiritual nourishment of the members of the People of God, the source for them of a life of faith, of hope and of love—and indeed a light for all humanity."[5]

But for that to happen, all who teach in religious education programs from pre-schoolers to adults should truly know what they are doing when they use the Bible. We know this is not the case, and it is not the Catechism of the Catholic Church which can help them in this matter because of the way it itself uses the Scriptures and because it seems that "the Catechism takes for granted, without spelling it out, that all its readers will be aware of the symbolic or figurative nature of much that is written there; that it is a book of words about the basically inexpressible; and that all its verbal symbols are interchangeable when the inexpressible requires expression." [6]

As Gerard Sloyan notes, most preachers and teachers are aware by now "about what not to say about it, how not to use it." But most are not really prepared to know how to use it. This is a very practical matter from the First Grade teacher who uses the Christmas and Epiphany narratives to the adult group that reflects on the Resurrection narratives. So there is a tremendous need for biblical formation for teachers at all levels. But there is also an urgent need, as I said before, to enable our young people to read, understand and interpret the Bible within our Catholic Tradition. This should be one of the main goals, it seems to me, of the search for cultural/theological religious literacy. [7]

b. The need to allow youth to participate more actively in their own education toward theological literacy and discipleship

To explain briefly this statement I will bring together some insights from three quite different sources: first, the document from the Pontifical Biblical Commission, second, a commentary by Joseph Jensen, and, third, an article by Michael Warren on youth evangelization. [8]

The Commission's document brings out clearly the need for a constant work of reinterpretation of the biblical texts both in the continuity of the Tradition and in the novelty brought about by each generation's effort in the actualization and inculturation of the Bible's message of life. [9] As Joseph Jensen rightly says, commenting on this topic: "New challenges confront the Church in each new age, and as the Church looks to the Scriptures for answers, new insights emerge from the age-old texts, and rightly so, for no single interpretation can exhaust the richness of what is often, necessarily, expressed in symbol and metaphor."[10]

Turning now to Michael Warren's article, I would like to focus on some of the insights he shares about youth evangelization today. Quoting research by Stanley Aranowitz and André Giroux,[11] Warren speaks about the "colonization" of the minds of the young by the powerful mass media culture we are living in. It is all the more dangerous that it is unconscious; they are colonized without being aware of it. In his mind this "subjugation of the spirit" calls for ". . . counterconditions for the cultural liberation of the young by means of a living out of a particular religious imagination—Muslim, Christian, Jewish, Hindu, Buddhist, and so forth." And he laments "that those counterconditions are far too little in place."[12] What the young would need, in other words, are "alternative visions of reality . . . harbored in alternative communities of discourse and life practice."[13] In plain language this means Christian communities where the young could truly be part of a "dialogue toward living out the meanings" that bind the community together. For sure youth ministry thrives on dialogue, but for Warren "this dialogue goes neither far enough nor deep enough." Let me quote him at length here because his comments are truly thought-provoking:

> In sometimes subtle ways, the churches ape society's way of dealing with the young. They expect the young to be consumers of the meaning system supposedly lived out by the church. Today, however, an important theological principle being recovered worldwide, especially by means of liberation theology, is that all persons have a right, indeed, a human duty, to become co-producers of religious meaning. This principle has yet to be applied widely to young people in local churches, or, for that matter, to laity of all ages.

Youth ministry efforts influencing young people toward discipleship do so because they allow the young to become co-producers of the religious culture in which they stand. And the efforts that are failing are those that reduce young people to the status of consumers, demanding that they accept doctrinal capital on a "handout" basis and then expecting them to put it to good use, i.e., to "invest" it in living practice.

Such a process is quite different from laying open to them the community's resources and inviting them to use these resources for engaging in the production of meaning: through dialogue, through struggling with the problematic of today's world, through allowing the questioning of assumptions, including doctrinal ones, found among many young people, and especially through action for justice. By participating actively in this religious culture as a co-producer, a person truly enters it as a zone of judgment exposing what is unacceptable in the wider culture.[14]

Isn't there a striking correspondence between the two needs just described: the need for the ancient texts of the Bible to be rediscovered and reinterpreted by each generation so that its riches of meaning and spiritual power for conversion and social transformation be fully deployed, and the need for the young to be invited to be co-producers of meaning for their time and their culture?

"Laying open the communities' resources and teaching them how to use them creatively to become co-producers of meaning"— isn't this what the search for cultural/theological religious literacy is all about? That kind of literacy will indeed help them to discover, to welcome the Reign of God in their own life experience and to continue growing over the years toward discipleship. And if the work involved in this young people's endeavor would be shared with the adult community, would it not be a wonderful enrichment for the whole community's life?

2. Curriculum Design

If they are understood properly and accepted, a holistic vision of and pastoral approach to religious education have very practical consequences on curriculum design. I will attempt to point out some of those consequences regarding three topics: the content, the process and the context.

A. The Content

The decisions concerning the scope and sequence of the overall curriculum will not be made with the obsession of completeness by the end of high school; they will be made in the light of the fundamental question I formerly proposed: "Which elements of our traditions, of our Catholic doctrine, which stories, poems, parables and excerpts from our Scriptures, which symbols and rituals from our liturgy, which stories from the past history of the Church and from its present activities in the world, might be the most assimilable, the most meaningful, the most life-giving for each stage of psychological development in today's world, in today's different cultures?" This means the criteria for choosing the themes will be relative to psychology, readiness and culture as much as to theology. And they will be concerned with enhancing spiritual life as much as with instruction.

This remark brings me to discuss an important topic which has been very fashionable in the last few years, i.e. lectionary-based regular catechetical programs. In this regard, I wish to make a clear distinction between the basic rhythm of the liturgical year and the lectionary. The seasons of the liturgical year have been for more than twenty-five years, and should remain, an important element in curriculum design. But I do not believe that the lectionary should be the basis for the scope and sequence of regular catechetical programs. I will not repeat the criticisms which have been made by very competent people like Tom Groome, Katherine Dooley, Robert Hater, Locker Bowman and many others. I agree with most of them.

However, for me, the question is not so much, "Is the lectionary enough to teach the whole tradition?" It is rather, "Is the lectionary the right food at the right time for the right people, namely, children and adolescents?" I sincerely believe it is not. Allow me to elaborate for a moment because this is of crucial importance.

I had the privilege many years ago, in my twenties, to work closely with Cardinal, then Father, Jean Daniélou in a Catholic Action movement. He had just written the foundational book, *Bible et Liturgie,* which deeply influenced both the liturgical and catechetical movements in Europe at that time. Later on, when I was teaching at Lumen Vitae, we were all enthused with what we then called Biblical and Liturgical Catechesis. So I have always been deeply committed to this type of catechesis. Indeed, when we wrote the *Come to the Father* series for Paulist Press in the late 1960s, this approach is what we tried to use. It was a contemplative and celebrative type of biblical catechesis in the early grades, and I probably lived the most wonderful experiences of my life teaching that program, especially in grades one and two.

Later on when I was teaching at Montreal University, I worked closely with a Dominican theologian and liturgist who is presently a member of the International Francophone Commission that is preparing the revision of the Roman Missal. His name is Guy Lapointe. He studied in Paris during the time the lectionary was being put together, and one of his teachers, Pierre Jounal, was on the committee completing the work. Discussing the lectionary with Father Lapointe at Montreal University recently, he told me this: "I can tell you one thing for sure. Not one of the people working on the lectionary ever dreamt it would be used as a basic text for the initiation of children." He believes as I do that to use the lectionary for the Christian initiation of children is a major distortion of its purpose.

I believe we have much work to do to find the best means to help our children appropriate the Bible gradually and deeply so that they will come back to it over a lifetime as a vital source of their growth in faith. Thirty years of experience have convinced me that when used appropriately, the Word of God can indeed become truly life-giving even for very young children, and remain so through adolescence and into adulthood. But like most of those who have worked with young children, such as Lubienska de Lenval, Sofia Cavaletti, Dr. Berryman and many others, I am convinced that the Bible stories, parables, poems and other texts have to be chosen with great care, according to children's readiness. The texts must be used in a way that respects the rhythms of children's spiritual growth and ways and pace of appropriation.

In my opinion, the lectionary is a straitjacket arbitrarily imposed on the initiatory journey of children that stifles the full potential of their spiritual growth. Some lectionary-based curriculums have achieved miraculous pedagogical acrobatics in dragging in and out of the lectionary very rich teaching. But in spite of the great talent of their authors, one constantly feels the contrived and artificial character of the journey—not because of the authors but because of the lectionary structure. One cannot but wonder, "Why on earth put oneself in such a rigid and contrived situation?"

I hate to seem to put down the work of the many catechists who are doing lectionary catechesis with great enthusiasm. But we must have the courage and honesty to ask ourselves: "Is this the best we can do for those whom we catechize? Is this the way to excellence in religious education in the long-run?" I sincerely believe it is not. Maybe we needed the transition through lectionary catechesis to become even more vividly aware of the Bible as a vital source of our catechetical work. I am convinced, however, that it is time to move on. And I wonder if ten years from now, we won't look back in amazement to this kind of "idolatry" of the lectionary!

Let the Liturgy of the Word achieve its full potential as the irreplaceable gathering of the community to hear, celebrate and appropriate the Word of God in the uniqueness of the liturgical setting. And let regular catechesis achieve its own potential in gradually, freely and gently opening up for our children the wonder-filled, rich diversity of our family treasure: the Bible. Let the children feast on the Word of God in their own way, at their own pace. Together, the Liturgy of the Word and regular catechesis will lead our children to conversion and discipleship, to a rich foundational religious literacy. Once again, it is not either/or but both, and each one in its time and place. Let me quote and paraphrase Kierkegaard again to close this topic: "I only know a truth when it has become life in me." I only know a Bible story, a parable, a quotation when it has become life in me. Here are two examples of what I mean.

When I was teaching *Come to the Father* in Grade One, the children enjoyed meditating and celebrating again and again certain quotations from the Bible that they regarded as especially meaningful because they were truly "Good News" to them. I remember a little girl who around the end of the year began writing the same quote day after day on her drawing book, whatever the topic of the lesson. The quote was from Isaiah 52:8–10: "I love you with an everlasting love; my love shall never turn away from you." When I asked her why she was doing that, she explained that her father had left home a few weeks ago, and those words of God gave her the courage to bear her terrible pain.

When I was teaching at Lumen Vitae, there was a wonderful catechist who used to meditate and play-act with the children carefully chosen parables from the Old and New Testaments. One of their favorites was the potter working the clay. She worked with six to eight year old children. During Advent that year, they decided to play-act the Annunciation. The little girl who was playing Mary's role blanked out when the time came for her to say, "Behold the handmaid of the Lord." She was silent for a moment; then she opened her hands and said with a smile: "I am in the hands of the Lord, like the clay in the hands of the potter" (Jer 18:1–6). Yes, indeed, carefully chosen words of God can become life in children's hearts! And the Bible should be, of course, at the very center of any catechetical program, but I believe the lectionary should not be the basis for their scope and sequence.

B. The Process

With regard to the process and materials I will propose a few comments on methodology and mention some concerns.

A holistic vision of religious education necessarily requires a participative pedagogy. Tremendous progress has been made in the last fifteen years or so in that respect, thanks to many wonderful books and authors, and in particular to the influence of Tom Groome's first book, *Christian Religious Education,* and more recently of the second one, *Sharing Faith.*

What these two books propose is in fact a very sophisticated theological and pedagogical elaboration of a basic and natural process[15] through which we instinctively relate our daily experiences and personal stories to our family values and traditions and to our cultural myths so as to understand ourselves, decide who we want to be and what we want to do. I find it also interesting to note that a pedagogical elaboration of that basic natural process for adult Christian education was first proposed at the beginning of this century by a Belgian priest, Father Joseph Cardijn, who founded in 1912 *La jeunesse ouvrière chrétienne* which would become later on in the English speaking world The Young Christian Workers movement. Its pedagogy was summed up in three key words: observe, judge, act. The judging, of course, was accomplished in the light of a prayerful meditation of the Gospel and a sharing of each one's insights.[16] Its aim was to help its members become true disciples in their own life, leaders, agents of change in their milieu. The movement began spreading in the U.S. around 1938 and mostly after the war. By then it had developed in various branches, such as the Young Christian Students and the Christian Family Movement. Their generic name was Catholic Action. I participated enthusiastically for many years in France in the Young Christian Student Movement. When I heard Thomas Groome speak of Shared Praxis for the first time at a Symposium I was part of at Boston College in 1978, it immediately rang a bell.

We should also acknowledge that even before Shared Praxis many catechetical programs had picked up on that "natural process" with the anthropological approach which had focused our attention on the life experience of the catechized. Those catechetical programs had encouraged a constant interaction between the child's experience and the Gospel with a hope of leading to a change of attitude and behavior. However the participative dimension of the process was often minimal or superficial.

The tremendous service Thomas Groome has rendered us especially in his second book is threefold:

- First, he offers us rich and profound philosophical and theological reflection on the foundations of that approach.
- Second, he proposes a very elaborate pedagogical enrichment of the approach and shows us how it can become a detailed methodology for teaching.
- Third, he enlarges the scope of the approach by suggesting how it can be beneficial in many other sectors of Christian ministry.

However I am not at all advocating the detailed methodology of Shared Praxis as the only adequate way to implement a holistic vision of religious education and participative pedagogy. What I am saying is that the original core of that approach, the constant interaction between the Christian traditions, mainly the Gospel and human experience in a participative process, is essential to a holistic way of doing religious education. The power of the process resides in that interaction. But it can be experienced in many different ways.

To end this section on process let me express two concerns: one has to do with the catechesis and the other with the catechists.

A holistic vision of religious education would require a much greater emphasis on the contemplative dimension of Christian life. Too often it seems to me that curriculums pay lip service to that aspect of the journey: a short prayer is suggested at the end of the lesson and that's it. The instruction is given much more time and value. But more importantly it is often the pervasive contemplative dimension of the whole process which seems to be lacking. Our curriculums are extremely busy; they don't seem to give the breathing space both the Spirit and the children need, not to mention the teachers! It seems as if we are afraid not to have enough things to do—but do we take the time just to be, to exist together intensely under the gentle touch of the Spirit in moments of quiet breathing, of silent questioning, of wondering, of meditating, of celebrating together? Instead of rushing in to our lessons to make sure we have time to "go through all the material," do we take the time to "care," as Maria Harris so beautifully explains,[17] preparing bodies and minds and hearts so that when the time comes something real can be born of the Spirit in the lives of those we teach? When a theme has been explored, related to our life and experience through sharing, and worked on through various activities, it seems to me it is of extreme importance also to take a leisurely time to celebrate it through meditation and prayer. This is not superfluous versus instruction. It is essential for the interiorization and appropriation in faith of what was taught. Incredibly dense moments of peace and joy in God's presence can be experienced in such celebrations.

But of course this can only happen if the catechists themselves are contemplative persons. This is why I believe that much greater attention should be given to that aspect of their formation. We are privileged to have on the market an abundance of wonderful books which can guide us toward a deeper spiritual life, a more contemplative way of being and of teaching. Among many others I would like to mention two which I feel can be especially helpful. The first is Padraic O'Hare's *The Way of Faithfulness*.[18] One of the merits of Padraic's book is that it will help catechists rediscover the very rich contemplative dimension in the classical works of two of our greatest authors in religious education theory: Gabriel Moran and Maria Harris. It will also briefly introduce them to the contemplative dimension of Judaism and of Eastern spiritualities. The other book I would like to recommend strongly for catechists' formation is *Sadhana*, by Anthony de Mello.[19] It is a very simple but powerful book for helping catechists discover at their own pace the paths of contemplation. Father de Mello's unique charism comes from his years of personal experience both in Eastern and Western Traditions as a practitioner as well as a spiritual director. His book can be used either individually or in small prayer groups. It could also be used in conjunction with videotapes bearing the same title and published by Tabor. Finally, may I also suggest that Part Four of the Catechism of the Catholic Church be used with the catechists; it is, in my opinion, the most useful part of the book for them to read and discuss as part of their spiritual preparation for their ministry. May I suggest, however, that books are only one of the means which can foster the formation of the catechists. Prayer groups, spiritual direction and days of recollection or annual retreats should also be considered.

C. The Context

As I said earlier it is the whole community that is responsible for the Christian initiation of new generations; that is why a pastoral approach is necessary if we are to be faithful to a holistic vision of religious education. Of course, curriculum designers are not solely responsible for the implementation of that approach, but they can do a great deal to create a context, an environment and a mentality in the catechists which will promote it. For instance, curriculums should be designed to allow great flexibility in the way they can be used, fostering small group activities allowing personal mentoring. Teachers' guides should encourage catechists to cooperate with other ministers in the parish with regard to the support given to parents, to the service dimension of the educational task, and to the children's formation in prayer and liturgical celebration, instead of trying to do or organize everything themselves. For instance, carefully selected adults from biblical groups or prayer groups could be asked to meet with the children, to share their experience and to invite those who are interested to form small groups of prayer, offering their help as guides in prayer. These people could also see to it that days of recollection or retreats could be offered to children and adolescents during the school year or the holidays.

The same thing could be done with adults involved in caring ministries who would agree to sponsor a child or small groups of children in their apprenticeship of Christian service. The liturgical team could offer interested children to participate in the preparation of the Sunday liturgies. This type of cooperative attitude, if it is truly encouraged in the teacher's guides and in their formation, could have a profound beneficial influence in the way religious education is done in a parish.

Appropriation to Life

- *What do you think of Francoise's distinction between "foundational existential religious literacy" (truths that are necessary to awaken faith and for personal relationship with God and must be assimilated as our own) and "cultural theological religious literacy" (e.g. knowing how to read the Bible)? Do you find it helpful?*

- *What of her comments on "lectionary based" catechesis? What is your position? Why do you take the position you do?*

- *How do you imagine nurturing your own ongoing realization of the "truths" of Christian faith? The contemplative aspect of your faith?*

Chapter Seven

Adult Education, Evangelization and Religious Practice

Focus for Reflection

For so long the Church thought of catechesis as something only for children. We were forgetting that God's desire for our growth into holiness of life is never-ending, that our hearts are always restless until they rest in God (St. Augustine). The journey of faith is lifelong, and is ever in need of being nurtured and educated. The developmental psychologists have amplified this point by describing "stages" in faith development that stretch from birth into eternity.

• *What do you see as the most crucial faith education needs of Catholic adults today?*

• *What are some of the ways that your parish tries to respond to these needs?*

• *How could we do far better with adult faith education? Let your imagination take off!*

When we want to reflect on adult education in the light of the paradigmatic shift we have described, we are rapidly confronted with very fundamental questions regarding Christian identity and its relationship with religious practice, the kind of Church we dream of, the style of community we want to build, the idea we have of sacraments and of the role they play in Christian life and in religious education. Many of these topics would deserve a whole book, and I would not have the competence to write it! However, I would like in the next two chapters to share a few thoughts about certain specific questions which concern me from a pastoral perspective.

Adult education is, of course, a huge field of activity, a thriving one in which the United States has been showing great leadership. I will briefly comment on a few points which I feel involve special risks and challenges. For the sake of clarity, I will distinguish three kinds of people or groups in the adult population of our parishes and neighborhoods:

• the so-called "practicing" Catholics, meaning, in our present state of mind, those who come regularly to the Eucharist;
• all the others whom we rarely or never see, who are either not baptized, not evangelized, not coming to Mass, or alienated from the Church;
• the third group includes individuals from the two preceding categories. They are the parents of the children who are in our religious education programs, especially those who ask for their children to receive the sacraments. We will discuss the special problems they face us with in the next chapter.

1. Practicing Catholics

Our ministry to practicing Catholics, which we will call a *pastoral ministry,* includes two aspects: one nurturing, the other prophetic.

The *nurturing* aspect calls for a variety of programs and other means aimed at helping people grow in faith, deepen their spiritual life and enrich their religious literacy. There is a variety of wonderful audio-visual resources and materials for this purpose, as well as a number of groups, movements and small communities doing great work in this area.

The *prophetic* or challenging aspect has its roots in the nurturing aspect but goes further. Its aim is to help practicing Catholics pass from the mentality of consumer to that of co-responsibility. It challenges them to discover their own call and charisms and to accept their share in the mission of the Church for the Reign of God as being part of discipleship. In this respect I don't think we have been quite as good, and I would like to suggest two ways we might improve.

First, it seems to me that a Shared Praxis approach to ministry is a very efficient way of gradually moving a community to become aware of its responsibilities and to take them on. In Part Three of Tom Groome's *Sharing Faith* one can find a wealth of very practical suggestions to do just that. When we can get a few people to come together around a topic, an event on a local, national or international scene, or a specific concern they share, the Shared Praxis approach is a wonderful tool to bring them to a much deeper reflection than they first imagined and eventually to involvment in some deliberate action.

Second, I believe there are many people of good will in our communities who are ready and even eager to do something to respond to that call, to assume their share of responsibility. However, they do not come forward because they are afraid they will be asked too much: too much for their abilities, their time or their self-confidence. The way to overcome this obstacle, this fear, is to make concretely clear to the community that there are a million ways for them to serve, involving limited time, using every possible gift, and in a variety of ministries.

Let us concentrate, for example, on the variety of ministries involved in the cooperative approach to religious education that we previously described. Apart from the ministry of the catechist, which requires special gifts for teaching plus a great deal of time because of the training, preparation, and meetings with the children and their families, there are a number of responsibilities that require much less time and for which one needs only a big heart and a desire to serve with a minimum of preparation. I like to call this the ministry of fellowship or of Christian friendship. Here are a few examples of this one-on-one fellowship ministry, which could enrich so much the overall religious education journey:

- Grandparents befriending young parents. They could just walk with them, listen to them, share their stories, encourage them in the pre-evangelization and evangelization phases and all along the religious education journey. Others might get in touch with parents on the occasion of their children's preparation for the sacraments to act as sponsors for a child and family.
- Adults befriending adolescents, at a time when they badly need personal relationships with significant adults outside of the family circle and of the school world.
- Those who are interested in peace and justice work or in caring ministries, or who are part of prayer groups might sponsor a child or adolescent in his or her learning experience of the Christian way of life.

Many people who are afraid of anything resembling teaching a class would be open to this kind of one-on-one fellowship ministry. Perhaps they would enjoy it so much they might little by little discover they can do more. Fostering this network of personal relationships is one very effective way of educating the adult community to its responsibility. In many parishes the RCIA, because of the great diversity in the forms of cooperation it requires, has been a major factor in awakening a community to its responsibilities.

2. The Unchurched or Alienated

When we come to the second section of population, the un-churched or alienated, we are talking more about an *evangelizing ministry* to the unchurched and a *healing ministry* to the alienated. Sometimes these overlap, sometimes they don't. Let us take a moment to better understand who are the people we are dealing with. They are of course very diverse. Some are quite sophisticated people who reject the authoritarian attitude of the Church in theological and moral matters but who continue on their own or within small communities to live an intense spiritual life and often a very dedicated life in the spirit of the Gospel. We will not deal with these people here but will turn our attention to those who are experiencing their alienation in a very different way. Allow me to share with you a memory and an insight which might help us understand them better.

About twenty-five years ago I had the privilege to enjoy a long conversation with Paul Ricoeur. We were discussing our common awareness that people in those days seemed to be indifferent to the foundational existential questions of meaning and purpose of life and death, which rendered any pastoral ministry very difficult. The myth of indefinite progress which would solve all our problems and the relatively prosperous life-style many enjoyed seemed to render most people spiritually numb; they didn't need God or salvation. Ricoeur said to me he thought that our main task should be to "reopen in people's minds and hearts a space for interrogation." I thought he was quite right, and my work with adults over the years was inspired by that insight. There are still people, especially among the wealthy business or showbiz class, who protect themselves from any existential questions through their unrelentless quest for more money, success and power. But in society at large the situation has evolved in a quite different direction.

The myth of indefinite progress is dead. Even if the cold war has ended, the world is in turmoil, many grave problems concerning the future of humankind weigh on our minds and hearts, and even the young generations are often feeling quite desperate. So the pastoral problem now is not so much that people don't have any questions, it is that they look for answers in all kinds of directions.

An ever increasing number of people wander away from the traditional churches and go from one sect or esoteric group or cult to the other in search of what they are missing to help them live a meaningful life. They are ready to follow any guru, to believe in spirits, in cosmic powers or energy, in extra-terrestrial beings, etc., and we know how sometimes their search ends in tragedy. There are over eight hundred such sects or groups in North America.

Moreover, these people who are spiritually uprooted live in a very troubled society. A few words will suffice to evoke it: violence, drugs, casual sex, teenage pregnancy, teenage suicide highest in the world in North America; remember that TV show in which teenagers were preoccupied with finding easy and sure ways to die instead of reasons for living? For most adults, especially parents, a hectic fragmented life. A constant struggle for so many to make ends meet. Both parents working, or single parents always out of breath, trying to survive all their responsibilities. What can we learn from those facts? Out of this global picture, let us draw a few simple statements which can direct our reflections:

- People do need to make sense of their lives.
- Deep down they are in search of a meaning, a purpose, a unity, a harmony for their lives.
- But they look elsewhere than to the Church for that meaning and that purpose. Why is that? There are many reasons, of course, and in particular the lack of meaningful supporting relationships within the community. But maybe one of the reasons is the way we deal with them when trying to evangelize them.

The great thrust in this country toward evangelization is wonderful. "From pews to shoes" is a great way to express it! But sometimes I fear that we might fall into old trappings in the form of a new clericalism. Clericalism remains a constant temptation in the Church. We are so concerned that our churches are empty and so eager to fill them up again that we might go about evangelization with a hidden agenda—namely, an unconscious, unspoken but dominant preoccupation to bring people back to Mass and fast! It might be interesting to ask ourselves two questions with regard to this overwhelming preoccupation. First, is it possible that it is rooted in an unconscious desire to reassure ourselves both about the inescapable necessity of coming to Mass every Sunday and about the success of our pastoral work when we have "brought people back"? The goal of going "from pews to shoes" would be to bring people back "from shoes to pews!"

The second question might be: Which idea of Christian identity, of Christian life underlies the urge to bring people back to Mass as a dominant priority? Would it be that for us a Christian is essentially someone who comes to Mass every Sunday? If we did have those ideas our evangelizing ministry would run the risk of being deeply biased. How can we avoid this trap, overcome this temptation? By going back to the Reign of God as the theological vision, the dominant image which must shape our evangelizing ministry. Let me explicate this briefly.

The Catechism of the Catholic Church in Section One of Part Three (page 424, n. 1699) describes in three powerful and dense lines our human vocation: "Life in the Holy Spirit fulfills the vocation of man." "This life is made up of divine charity and human solidarity. It is graciously offered as salvation." It seems to me that this description is very close to what I tried to say about the Reign of God: a gracious gift of love enabling us to live in communion with God and in solidarity with others in the manner of Jesus. This is the dominant image, the point of reference we should have in mind when dealing with questions of adult education, of evangelization and of Christian identity. This is what religious practice is about: life in communion with God and in solidarity with others. What is the place of the Eucharist in this total picture? This is what we will focus on in the next chapter; but for now let us return to evangelization.

Evangelization is a pervasive reality. It can happen in an infinite variety of ways, times and places. Evangelization is not only a specific ministry, but a way of being for a community and for each of its members within the neighborhood. As Christians—and even more as catechists or pastors—we are constantly evangelizing or counter-evangelizing simply by the way we deal with people, especially parents. As Christians, our relationships have a kind of sacramentality to them. We are either revealing or hiding the mystery of God's love. For many people, we will perhaps be the only Gospel they will ever read, the only Gospel through which they might get a glimpse and taste of what the Reign of God is about. Indeed, the medium is the message, and the medium is the people.

Evangelization, then, is first of all a way of relating to people. But it is also a ministry. Let me elaborate a little on what I believe the very first step should be in that ministry if we don't want it to be only the sharing of an ideology or a recruitment campaign. If evangelization, as well as religious education, is to be authentic, it has to reach people to the "core of their being," as Robert Hater recently wrote in an excellent article on that topic, because this is where Revelation happens in our lives. Two great authors have profoundly enriched my thinking and deepened my conviction about this over the years: Karl Rahner and Gabriel Moran. I hope I will not betray them in trying to explicate that conviction.

When through our own personal experience we come in touch with the depth of reality, it reveals itself as relational, as open to the possibility of an unnamed presence, which is most often perceived as benevolent. As Gabriel Moran used to say, it is because reality is relational that it is revelatory. According to Rahner, what we do in our evangelizing or educational ministries is "assist understanding of what has already been experienced in the depth of human reality as grace (i.e. as in absolutely direct relation to God)."[1] If this is true, then our very first task is to encourage people to reach down to the core of their being, to the depth of reality where the ultimate questions can rise, where our contingency can be vividly experienced and where revelation can happen under the touch of the Spirit. Only then can faith eventually awaken when this inner revelation is freely welcomed in one's heart and mind. Only then will the words of faith we share with that person become truly meaningful because they will name Someone who has already been mysteriously encountered, and explicate what has already been intuitively perceived. Only then will they be ready to truly hear the Good News: that God's love is unconditional, that it is a free gift inviting them to enter into God's reign of love by living in communion with the Trinity and in solidarity with all creatures in their daily life.

So, what is essential at this stage is not formally teaching the doctrine, or involving people in any kind of process, or bringing them to Mass. It is encouraging the development of a personal relationship with God through prayer, through moments of aware-ness; in other words, it is the contemplative dimension of the Christian life which comes first, and flowing from it the first efforts to truly love as Jesus did in the ordinariness of daily life.

Letting people enjoy at their own pace this first experience and taste of the Reign of God is crucial in these early stages of our ministry of evangelization. For many people it will take time to discover and experience that the parish is indeed where commu-nion with God and with one another can be nourished and cele-brated. It might take a long time for some people to journey from the domestic Church, to the small community Church, to the large parish Church. We should let them take that time. This does not mean that the Eucharist is not important for me; on the contrary, as I will explain in the next chapter, the Eucharist is a foundational symbolic reality which is at the very heart of Christian life and Christian education.

However, in our evangelizing ministry to those adults who have only started their journey to or back to the Church, we should follow the lead of the Spirit, and not precede her. We should help people take the step they are ready for, and not push them to do more. We should also never forget what Anthony de Mello used to say: "The important distinction in our religion is not between those who practice and those who do not, but between those who truly love and those who do not." Was he not echoing the very words of John: "That we have passed from death to life, we know because we love our brothers" (1 Jn 3:14). "Whoever does not love cannot know God (should we add: even if he or she is coming to Mass every Sunday?) for God is love" (1 Jn 4:8). "God is love, and he who abides in love abides in God, and God in him" (1 Jn 4:16).

If we help people discover at their own pace the gift of God's love and the revitalizing power of a life of communion with God in faith and prayer, and of solidarity with others, one day they will want, they will need, to celebrate that communion in their community's liturgy. It will be up to us then to offer them celebrations which are truly meaningful and life-giving. So maybe the "practice" we should be concerned about in our evangelizing ministry is not so much—and definitely not predominantly—participation in the Sunday Eucharist, but openness of the heart through faith and prayer to the gift of God's love, to the joy of the Kingdom, which some day will bring them to the Table, because they will hunger and thirst for a deeper communion.

Appropriation to Life

• *Think of a person with whom you would like to share your vibrant Christian faith (either as new to him or her, or inviting a "cradle" Christian to let his or her faith "come alive" again).*

What style or approach will you use?
How will you initiate the conversation?
What is the "core" that you will share?
What from this chapter might help you?

• *Will you "engineer" such an encounter and give it a try?*

Chapter Eight

The Place and Role of the Eucharist in a Holistic Vision of Religious Education

Focus for Reflection

It is said that St. Augustine of Hippo often finished his cele-bration of Mass by saying to the congregants: "Go and be-come what you have received—the Body of Christ." The very word Mass comes from the Latin missa, *which means to be "sent." At the end of the Eucharist, we are always com-*missio-*ned anew to go and "love and serve"—to live what we have received and celebrated.*

* *Looking at your own daily life, what are some of the "every-day" things that it means for you to "live the Eucharist"?*

* *What are some things in our society, even in our Church, that make it difficult for us to live the Eucharist?*

* *What are some things that can help us to live it?*

In the past years there has been a renewed insistence on the central importance of the Eucharist as the "source and summit" of our Christian life. Of course, I agree with that statement, but I would like to propose my own interpretation of its meaning. Let me first share with you two concerns which led me to include this topic in the book.

First, an educational concern about our teaching ministry: Are we putting too much emphasis on the Eucharist as a liturgical *celebration* and not enough on the Eucharist as a *mystery of communion* with God and with one another which is to be experienced and celebrated in our daily life if it is to be authentically, genuinely celebrated in the community? Second, a pastoral concern, which I mentioned in the preceding chapter about our evangelizing ministry: Are we over-preoccupied with "bringing people back to Mass" rather than helping them discover the gift of the Reign of God, of God's loving presence at the heart of their own being and in the ordinariness of their daily life? I will attempt to address these concerns in reflecting with you on two topics: how the two rituals Jesus performed during his Last Supper—the washing of the feet and the breaking of the bread—enlighten one another; what it means, concretely, to experience and celebrate the mystery of the Eucharist in our daily life.

1. How do the two rituals Jesus performed enlighten one another?

Let us go back for a moment to the Last Supper in a meditative mood. That meal which Jesus shared with his disciples before his death was not an esoteric farewell ritual cut-off from his past life; it symbolized the essence of what his life had been; it ritualized what he had experienced and lived all along. Day by day during his whole life, the Word who became flesh had tried to embody, to make visible God's love for the world. He had done this not only by sharing his own experience of God's love, but also by curing the sick, fighting injustice, defending the poor, and opposing the religious leaders who oppressed the people under the burden of the Law.

Because he had given his life day by day for this cause, he was led to a point in the historical context of his time where the repressive forces which he had opposed were closing in on him. Jesus sensed this, and before they got to him, he sought to sum up the meaning and purpose of his life and his approaching death in one symbolic gesture. He did this in the context of the Passover Meal, celebrating God's saving, liberating actions of the past, so that what he was about to do would be understood in the same context.

When he took the bread and wine in his hands, it was his whole life he was holding, a life of love offered day by day. It was also his death which he anticipated and accepted. As he had said earlier, "No one takes my life away. I give my life." In this ritual he summed up the meaning and purpose of his life and his death. First, Jesus gave thanks for the Father's love and for the gift of his own life. Then he gathered in his offering all his past life of love and his imminent death: "This is my body . . . this is my blood . . . this is my *life* given up for you." When Jesus said after that: "Do this in memory of me," he did not mean only: "Perform this ritual in memory of me." He meant much more; he meant: "Do as I did. Give your life day by day and even unto death. And find there, as I did, the meaning and purpose of your life and your death." But Jesus also meant, of course: *Come together to celebrate this meal in memory of me. For this is where you will find the discernment and courage you will need to walk in my footsteps, to give your life as I did, day by day.*

Let me point out here the fundamental link between this eucharistic ritual which the three Synoptics report to us and another ritual, a baptismal ritual, which according to John preceded it: the washing of the feet. To fully understand the spiritual richness of the eucharistic ritual we must replace it in the context of John's chapters 13 to 18, that is, between the washing of the feet and the Last Discourse which explicates the full meaning of both rituals. As Bruno Barnhart explains in his recently published masterpiece, *The Good Wine*,[1] those two rituals powerfully symbolize the end

of the "old world" where power and domination were the order of
the day, and the beginning of the "new world" where humility and
love would be the order of the day. Let us take a moment to recall
in meditation this awesome ritual.

The mood is solemn and grave. Jesus is fully aware both of
Judas' betrayal and of his impending death:

> Before the feast of Passover,
> Jesus realized that the hour had come for him
> to pass from this world to the Father.
> He had loved his own in this world
> and would show his love for them to the end. . . .
> Jesus—fully aware that he had come from God
> and was going to God,
> the Father who had handed everything over to him—
> rose from the meal and took off his cloak.
> He picked up a towel and tied it around himself.
> Then he poured water into a basin
> and began to wash his disciples' feet
> and dry them with the towel he had around him (Jn 13:1–6).

Slowly reading this text can we not feel almost physically the
incredible density of the silent amazement which must have filled
the room while the disciples followed every gesture of Jesus until
he came to Peter? And the commentary, the catechesis Jesus gives
of his gesture is just as solemn:

> "Do you understand what I just did for you?
> You address me as 'Teacher' and 'Lord,'
> and fittingly enough, for that is what I am.
> But if I washed your feet—
> I who am Teacher and Lord—
> then you must wash each other's feet.

What I just did was to give you an example:
as I have done, so you must do" (Jn 13:12–16).

I believe we should interpret the words of Jesus "Do this in memory of me" in the light of those other words, "As I have done, so you must do." The first ritual enlightens the second; it brings out the focus of this Last Supper: "This is my life given up for you. Do as I did, walk in my footsteps." And the Last Discourse echoes repeatedly in many different forms what is the essence of a disciple's life, of a eucharistic life: a life of communion with God and of solidarity with one another:[2]

"I give you a new commandment: love one another.
Such as my love has been for you,
so must your love be for each other.
This is how all will know you for my disciples:
your love for one another" (Jn 13:34–36).

"As the Father has loved me
so I have loved you.
Live on in my love.
You will live in my love
if you keep my commandments,
even as I have kept my Father's commandments,
and live in his love.
All this I tell you that my joy may be yours
and your joy may be complete" (Jn 15:9–13).

Bringing together those two sacred rituals and the Last Discourse helps us understand that the Eucharist is indeed a mystery of communion with God and of solidarity with one another, which is to be experienced and celebrated in our daily life if it is to be authentically celebrated in the liturgy. So the heart of the Eucharist as *mystery* of faith in which we share is this: it is Jesus continuing to give thanks to the Father and to give his life through each and every one of the members of his Body, through each and every one of us day by day. Since the Incarnation we are inseparable from Jesus; we are One Body.

And the Eucharist as *celebration* is the community of Christians coming together to give thanks for, to celebrate and to actualize sacramentally this ongoing eucharistic mystery in their lives, which was inaugurated in the death and resurrection of Jesus and the outpouring of the Spirit. Christian life is radically and fundamentally a eucharistic life, a life of communion with God and of solidarity with others. Is it not essential that we understand this thoroughly if we are to truly grasp what evangelization is about, what Christian education and sacramental preparation are about? So let us now reflect on a second question.

2. What does it mean, in concrete terms, to live the Eucharist?

First, a preliminary remark. As we said earlier, people do need to make sense of their lives. Deep down they are in search of a meaning, a unity, and a purpose for their hectic, fragmented lives. But often they look elsewhere than to our Church for that meaning and purpose. There are many reasons for that, of course. One of them, however, seems to me that the various groups or churches that people are attending not only offer a global vision of the world, they also help the people relate it to their daily lives, make sense of their daily lives. They do so through various means, but two in particular. They propose daily rituals which are linked to the communal ones, and encourage basic attitudes through which this global vision gets a hold on people's lives. For us however, our vision of faith, our Sunday Eucharist and our daily life too often have almost no link. As Father Patrick Brennan puts it, people come to church on Sunday to "get their holy thing and their Sunday paper and go home to unchanged lives." Mass is a parenthesis; although it is holy, it remains a parenthesis!

But this is not inevitable. So let us see how we can help people live the Eucharist, or, putting it another way: how the mystery of the Eucharist can deeply transform and shape our life if we truly welcome it into our heart. To simplify and summarize greatly, let us say it does it in two ways: first, it offers us an overall vision of the meaning and purpose of our lives; second, if we accept that vision, it awakens in us two basic attitudes which will shape our lives.

First, the vision. In the mystery of the Eucharist we are vividly reminded of the fundamental meaning of our life and of its overall purpose. We are reminded that our life is a gift of love whose final aim is to enable us to live in communion with God, to share in God's own life and happiness eternally. We are reminded that this can only happen if we freely accept to walk in the footsteps of Jesus, by giving our life as he did, thus sharing in the Great Story of God's love for the world and building the Reign of God. This then is the global vision in which we find the overall meaning and purpose of the whole universe, of the whole human history and of each one of our individual lives.

Second, the attitudes. If we accept it, this vision of the sacredness, of the eucharistic dimension of our daily life awakens in us the two fundamental eucharistic attitudes which will shape our lives:

a) gratefulness of the heart, a disposition to receive our life as a gift of love, day after day, and receive it with a thankful heart;
b) openness of the heart, a disposition to offer, to share our life as a gift of love as Jesus did: "This is my life . . . my life of today, given for you . . . so that in this world, today, the kingdom of love may grow. . . . "

So what does it mean to live the Eucharist? It means interpreting our life, day after day, in the light of the Reign of God, and letting our life be shaped day after day by the two main eucharistic attitudes: thankfulness, gratefulness of the heart, openness of the heart, willingness to give our life and not only live our life, and finding in that way of life an exhilarating sense of purpose, a conviction that we do indeed make a difference in the world, that everything in our life is bearing fruit for the salvation of the world.

But for this vision of faith to truly get a hold on our life there is a prerequisite; I will name it with different traditions in many different ways to help us understand what it is. We need spiritual aliveness, or interiority, or mindfulness, or awakeness, or what Anthony de Mello called awareness.[3] When he was asked what is awareness, Tony used to say: "If you've experienced it, you don't need a definition. And if you haven't you would not understand the definition!" As usual he borrowed a saying from the East to try to explain it: "In the East people don't say God created the world, they say, *God dances the world.*" The dance and the dancer are not the same; but they are inseparable. And he said: "Might it be possible that we see the dance, but not the dancer?" Awareness, then, would be to see the dancer and not only the dance! And Tony added: "If you look at a tree and see a tree you have really not seen the tree. When you look at the tree and see a miracle, then, at last, you have seen!"

Let us then think of awareness as a capacity, an ability to see through reality, to sense the mysterious dimension of reality which for us is the pervasive presence and action of God, the dancer! Awareness is opposed to superficiality or exteriority, or spiritual numbness; it is the contemplative way of being, which opens in our heart the eyes of faith. But for the eucharistic attitudes to get a hold on our life we need something else—we need rituals.

Rituals are a fundamental aspect of our humaneness; they allow us to relate humanly to ourselves, to others, to the world, to God. Any relationship, any community needs rituals to simply exist, then to last and to grow. It is also through rituals that we need to express the meaning we give to our life. If our life is to be something else than the hectic, superficial, fragmented "running around" we talked about, then the awareness, the vision of faith of our life as eucharist, must find its concrete expression in daily rituals, linked to the biological rhythm of our life; otherwise that vision cannot get a hold on our real life. Every religion has understood that and Christianity is no exception. But unfortunately we have somewhat lost sight of the relevance, significance and power of those traditional rituals; or, if they are still used, they are often superficial and mechanical, taken over by routine. I am talking here of course about morning and evening prayer as the anchor-points, the foundational pillars of a eucharistic life all along the day.

Let us look for a moment at our life and the different ways we can begin our day. As soon as we get up we can let ourselves be overwhelmed by the million worries, tasks, responsibilities of the coming day, and begin the rat race, rushing to the bathroom, to the kids' room, then the kitchen, etc.; the day has hardly begun and we are already out of breath. Or we can begin our day by taking ninety seconds or so to "look at the dancer" before we rejoin the dance of creation. We don't even need words. We might stand barefoot on the floor, feeling the ground of our planet earth under our feet. We breathe slowly and deeply, letting the Spirit fill our heart as the air fills our lungs. We become present to God who is always present to us. Then we might slowly open our arms in moving them upward, expressing our praise, our thanksgiving and our offering in communion with Jesus, then extending our arms wide open to the dimension of the universe, of the whole human family with which we are one, praying for the Kingdom to come![4]

I am deeply convinced that such a ritual, in its simplicity, or any other similar one—provided we truly inhabit it, put ourselves wholeheartedly in it—can have a far-reaching and even decisive effect on the human and Christian quality of our day. In it we are renewing our communion with God and with the whole creation, we are all at once expressing our thankfulness and our praise for the gift of our lives, our willingness to live with an open heart, accepting whatever may come, and trying to give our life through everything we do. We are saying with Jesus: "This is my life given for you. . . ." And we are saying this to our spouse if we have one, to our children, our students, our colleagues, all the people we will meet during that day. That moment of awareness, that offering will be the golden thread giving its unity and meaning to our fragmented day; it will be the first ritual of our daily eucharist. All the rest of our day the relationships, the work, the success and the failures, the happiness and the brokenness, all that will be precious as gold, will be eucharist, part of the Great Story of God's love for the world; all that will be making the Kingdom grow and building a better world, a world as God wants it to be.

Once in a while, perhaps, during the day, for a fleeting moment, we will "see the dancer" again; it can happen anytime, anywhere. But we should do nothing constrained, just remain open, quiet in our heart, and the Spirit will gently lead us to live our life in its depth, in awareness, or, as Tony used to say, "to listen to the song in our heart." There is no duality there, one eye on what we are doing, one on the Lord; remember, the dance and the dancer are one. God never asks us to squint. But we simply discover more and more that we are inseparable from God, that God is never elsewhere than where we are. So our daily eucharist goes on, from home to work, back home from the neighborhood; we have joined the Dancer in the dance.

Then evening comes, and we will try to make the last moments we spend together quality moments of sharing and caring, perhaps forgiveness, reconciliation and peace if needed. We will end our eucharist for the day with another simple ritual: putting our life in God's hands, giving thanks for the day, laying down with our tired body our concerns, our worries, our unfulfilled dreams, unfinished tasks, our shortcomings and our sins, trusting in God's love. All is well for today, the Mass is ended, may our heart rest in peace! Tomorrow the dance will continue.

I am deeply convinced that if we are to truly live a Christian life, we need those simple daily rituals to keep alive our awareness of the real depth, the true meaning, the rich purpose of our life. Yes indeed, "the Eucharist is source and summit" of our Christian life provided we see it as a mystery of communion with God and of solidarity with one another, as well as a liturgical celebration. And how important for us to present this holistic vision to adults and children alike in our evangelizing and catechetical ministries, rather than being over-preoccupied with bringing them to Mass as soon as possible.

Our liturgists will probably tell us that if we bring people back to a liturgy that is wonderful and vibrant, they will discover meaning for their lives. Certainly this would work for some people, perhaps for many—provided, of course, that our liturgies are such. But in today's context and for the majority of people, it will not work. Not only will they not come but many also feel excluded because of their life-style. I believe that rather than urging people to come back to Mass we should help them through our evangelizing ministry to discover, understand and appreciate the fact that the essential mystery of the Eucharist, which can give meaning, purpose and unity to our lives, is to be experienced and celebrated at the heart of our daily life, family life, work life, and social activities day-by-day. It is from this experience that the desire and need to join in the community's sacramental celebration of the Eucharist will emerge.

This should apply especially to the parents who come to us asking for their children to receive a sacrament. A great majority of them are not practicing Catholics for various reasons. Many dread the mandatory requirement of "their coming to Mass" which we sometimes link to the sacramental preparation of their children. Making things mandatory is not a lasting solution: as one mother said to a friend after the parents' meeting: "I'll go through all the gimmicks they want just so my little girl can make her First Communion!" Gently helping people discover how meaningful things can be is, in my opinion, a better solution.

Celebrating the eucharistic meal only becomes deeply meaningful when it brings together, unifies and celebrates in the community what has been experienced of God's saving love in day-to-day living. As Bernard Lee says, "When ritual meaning and daily meanings do not intersect the absurdity is thundering." I believe the Eucharist is a mystery of communion which should be experienced in daily life, if it is ever to be celebrated authentically in the community.

So what does it mean in simple concrete terms to help people discover and experience the mystery of the Eucharist in their daily lives? It means helping them discover the loving presence of God and the infinite value and price of their own life—just as it is—when it is lived in communion with Jesus. It means inviting them to *welcome* their life as a gift of love every day and to *give thanks for it*. It means inviting them to *offer* their life, just as it is, with its daily struggles and tasks, its failures, its joys and its pains, its fulfilling or troubled relationships. It means inviting them to do their best *to live ordinary, nitty-gritty life with an open heart, a loving, forgiving heart*—and knowing, believing that in doing that, *they are giving their life with Jesus.* They are indeed *sharing in the eucharistic mystery* which gives unity, meaning and purpose to our lives.

Indeed, the mystery of the Eucharist is where the *totality* of our life and its *dailiness* finds its purpose, meaning and unity. If we gently, one step-at-a-time, help people understand and experience this, they will gradually begin to realize that they are indeed part of the Christian community. Thus, when we invite them to join us in celebrating the life we share, perhaps they will want to come. This approach is especially important for those many parents who, because of their situation, cannot share in the eucharistic bread, and therefore feel rejected. You wouldn't believe how some of them who have discovered this insight come to life again, spiritually; they feel they belong again. Just a few weeks ago, a mother of four in a blended family embraced me and said, with tears in her eyes, "You don't know what you've done for me; I feel resurrected!" And maybe it is those people who will help our liturgies become more and more what they are supposed to be: the life-giving gatherings of real communities where people come to give thanks for all of God's gifts and to learn how to share them in love, instead of fighting over them. Isn't it exactly what humankind needs today? Isn't it what the Reign of God is about?

Appropriation to Life

- *What do you think of Francoise's suggestion to begin and end each day with a brief ritual to encourage a sense that all life is to be lived as Eucharist?*

- *What such ritual might you find helpful to give a sense of sacramentality to your every day?*

- *Will you try it tomorrow?*

PART THREE

AWAKENINGS: THE UNIQUE IMPORTANCE OF THE BEGINNINGS

❖

❖

A holistic vision of religious education inspired by the Reign of God as its dominant image and its metapurpose should have a very profound and precise influence on early childhood education. Indeed if the beginnings are not shaped by that vision, the further development of the child may be not only hindered but lastingly deformed. Psychology teaches us that by age five or six all the basic structures of the personality—the outlook on life, the relational style, etc.—are in place. This is true also for the religious life of the child. That is why I would like to end this book by sharing some reflections on this topic which is especially dear to my heart.

When we talk about parents ministering to their children, most people immediately think about teaching religion to the children. But this is only a very small part of what ministering to our children is about. I propose that we reflect on a much broader, more profound and more foundational reality. We are all familiar with Saint Irenaeus' saying: "The glory of God is man fully alive." Could we not transpose this quote in saying: "The glory of parents is children fully alive"? In that light I submit to you that parents' ministry to their children is to help them become fully alive not only physically, intellectually and emotionally, but also spiritually and morally.

More than fifty years ago Maria Montessori talked about the "spiritual embryo" in every newborn child, and she worried that even then, in the modern culture of her time, this embryo would not be given the chance to fully develop, thus mutilating our children in an essential dimension of their humanity. How much more worried she would be today in our post-modern culture!

So we will focus our attention now on what seems to me to be the essential task of parents with regard to the development of the spiritual embryo in their children. I believe that task is first and foremost to lay the foundations so the spiritual potential of their children may not only be preserved but enhanced, nourished, strengthened and enriched over the years. We will center our reflections around three questions:

- What are the main dynamic components of that spiritual embryo? Our perspective then will be psychological. It will be presented in Chapter Nine.
- How can we encourage in the home a healthy development of these components? Here we will be concentrating on educational perspectives which will be discussed in Chapter Ten.
- What do parents need to live up to the challenge of their task as nurturers of their children's spiritual life? Here we will discuss very briefly some pastoral perspectives which will also be presented in Chapter Ten.

Chapter Nine

The Awakening of Faith and Longing for God From a Psychological Perspective

Focus for Reflection

One of the loveliest writings of the great Irish poet William Butler Yeats is entitled "The Land of Heart's Desire." This "land" is a deeply spiritual place, because, as Ignatius of Loyola was convinced, the deepest desires of our hearts signal to us the movements of God's Spirit in our lives. Our best desires signal God's desire—God's "will"—for us.

- *What are some of the deepest and most life-giving desires of your own heart at this time?*

- *Try to trace the source of those desires. Are they from God? To what is God inviting you?*

- *What do you remember or imagine as the deepest desires of children? How can those desires be engaged catechetically for their spiritual awakening?*

What are the main dynamic components of the spiritual embryo in the child? This of course is a fascinating and very complex question. It is related all at once to philosophy, metaphysics, anthropology, psychology and theology. The experts in these different fields often disagree even on the meaning of the words they use to discuss it! So I will have to simplify drastically their ideas, and we will focus on three of these dynamic components: the longing for happiness, the sensitivity to the numinous which means the sacred or the holy, or what some call the religious awareness or intuitive knowledge of the divine in the child, and finally the search for meaning.

1. The longing for happiness

To understand what this is about we should ask ourselves questions like the following:

- Where is the birthplace, the source of human desire, drive, longing for happiness?
- What is the foundational experience from which is born human desire?

From a philosophical point of view Plato answered this question in *The Banquet* and in *Phedre.* For him human longing is born of riches and poverty (*poros* and *penia*). It inhabits the human heart, linking it to the gods; it is both human and divine.

From a psychological point of view and on a more personal level we might ask ourselves another question: What is our very first, primordial, global experience of happiness, of total, pervasive well-being? It is our oneness with our mother in her womb, before our birth, and in the warmth of her loving arms after we are born. It is the tenderness and care that surround our first weeks and months in life (*poros*).

What is our very first desire, urge, drive when we are separated (*penia*) from that primordial, archaic, blissful experience after we are born? To recover it at once, to be totally immersed in it again, to lose ourselves in it forever.

What is the very first challenge we face in life? Having to learn how to renounce that urge of "going back to our lost paradise" so we can follow the call of life, the call to grow, to go forth, to risk moving into the unknown, into the future, into freedom and responsibility. And how are we brought to face that challenge? Through confrontation with reality, that reality being mainly the father, and eventually brothers or sisters with whom we are forced to share the mother and to learn to wait for the gratification of her presence, thus learning to accept the reality of time and the reality of others.[1]

The tremendous psychological energy in this primordial urge, desire, longing for total happiness, is called "Eros." (Let us not be mistaken—sexual and genital eroticism is only one aspect, one dimension of that energy.) Eros is the wonderful power energizing our total psychological growth, provided we don't let it turn back on itself in search of an archaic, narcissistic and illusive nirvana. If we are ever to develop a wholesome personality, a healthy emotional life, a real autonomy, a capacity for true love and free communion with others and eventually with God, we have to be willing to renounce this urge of "going back to," and turn our desire, our longing to the future, seeking another kind of happiness, of oneness, which will have an altruistic character, accepting others as others to be respected and loved. We will thus be overcoming our fundamental temptation of narcissism and egocentrism, and opening ourselves up to "agape," using the energy of Eros.

So the first dynamic component of the spiritual embryo in the child is Eros, the powerful energy of our longing, of our thirst for happiness, evolving from the foundational, primordial, diffuse experience of happiness in loving oneness with our mother. But we must go further and recognize with Antoine Vergote—an eminent scholar both in psychology and theology—that "though desire for God may completely transform Eros, it nevertheless arises from

it."[2] So the question we will look into now is: How can this transformation occur? This brings us to the second dynamic component
of the "spiritual embryo" in the child.

2. The sensitivity to the "numinous," or the sacred, the holy

It is widely recognized now by psychologists, educators and
theologians that there is in children an innate sensitivity to the
mysterious dimension of reality. Some speak of poetic sensitivity,
others of religious awareness. Whatever the names, they all refer
to the capacity of children—very young children—for what we can
call, in a broad, general sense, intuitive, affective religious experience. Indeed, if we had no intuition of God, how could we ever
search for God, long for communion with God? How could God's
Word reach the human heart if there was not in that heart an innate
capacity to "hear" that Word, to be touched and "awakened" by it?[3]

In a wonderful little book—well known by now—Edward
Robinson spoke of the "original vision" of children.[4] That original
vision and experience is a very rich one: it is made up of feelings
of wonder and awe, of intuitive knowledge or what Tillich called
"numinous astonishment," of feelings of oneness with all things,
and of personal significance (which of course can only much later
in life be recognized and named as such). Psychology helps us to
recognize the source of this experience in two aspects of the child's
psychological structure: animism and religious imagination.

For the very young child, as for adults in some so-called primitive cultures, everything is alive, everything is the epiphany of a
mysterious presence. This is the source of many enchanting experiences, as we can see in Robinson's book. I remember a little six
year old girl, who had begun experiencing short night walks in the
country during a vacation, telling me with exhilaration: "It's
wonderful! When I take a walk at night the moon follows me everywhere, everywhere!" Haven't we all had the opportunity to expe-

rience our "inner child" being reawakened in wonder when taking a walk with a child or sitting together quietly, wrapped in amazement, looking at an animal, a plant, a sunset or the sea? In such moments the child helps us rediscover the world as a gift of love.

But this animism can also be the source of frightening experiences, and we must understand them if we are to help the child overcome them. Gertrud Mueller Nelson, in her wonderful book *To Dance with God,* has a delightful story about a raging boar in a picture book which fascinated little Peter. As long as it was daylight and the boar was in the book Peter enjoyed tremendously looking at it; he had control over it. But at night the boar became very much alive and came to visit Peter in his room. And it took Mom and Dad a week to get rid of the boar once and for all![5]

What comes out strongly in Robinson's book is that generally in children's original vision the world is both awesome and benevolent. What is most significant is that this intuitive and affective experience of the unnamed mysterious presence which is perceived as pervasive to reality seems to be somewhat linked to and shaped by the earlier experiences of happiness, tenderness, security and well-being which give birth to Eros. It is as if these earlier primitive experiences colored to its depth the child's first intuitive religious awareness and perception of the universe. In other words, because of the conjunction of these various elements—the primordial experiences of love and happiness, the child's animism, intuitive perception of the divine and religious imagination—the child's first apprehension or perception both of the universe and of God is a positive, benevolent, peaceful, happy one.

But there is unfortunately a dark side to this reality; it lies in the fact that when this foundational, primitive experience of happiness, love and tenderness is lacking, then the intuition of our personal significance as well as our integration in a benevolent "Whole" cannot truly develop. This has a deeply negative effect on the child's spiritual development: "If he has not had the early experience of happiness, the subject will be cut off from the source of religious desire. If Eros has not been able to blossom out, man is deprived of this imaginative and affective power which makes him capable of the symbolic perception of the world."[6]

The works of Jean-Paul Sartre vividly illustrate the preceding statements: "I lived in terror. . . . I felt I was too much, so I had to disappear; I was a washed out blossom threatened with perpetual extinction. . . . God might well have dragged me out of trouble: I might have been a signed masterpiece; assured of holding my part in the universal concert, I might have waited patiently till he showed me his plans and my need. I had a presentiment of religion. I hoped for it; it was the remedy. . . . But following on that, in the fashionable God I learned about, I did not recognize whom my soul awaited: I needed a Creator, they gave me a Big Boss; the two were only one but I did not know that; I served without warmth the pharisaical Idol, and the official doctrine disgusted me in the search after my own faith."[7]

This powerful text dramatically brings out the traumatic effect of early affective deprivation on the personality itself and on religious development. That is why it is tragic that so many children experience it. However I believe there is still hope for those children, because the power of the Spirit can work through even these negative conditions to awaken the spiritual life of the child if he or she later on finds help through meaningful relationships and experiences. This might happen during adolescence or even much later in life when circumstances force us to face the ultimate limits and questions of our humaneness.

3. The third component of the spiritual embryo: the search for meaning

We are more used to notice this component because its manifestations are more obvious in the sempiternal use of the words "why" and "how."

There is an incredible mental activity in the young child. But the child's mind does not function like ours in abstract reasoning and logic. Children have their own way of making sense of their life and of the world around them. Even when we answer their questions they have their own way of rearranging the data, which sometimes gives amazing results when we are lucky enough to hear them repeat to a younger child what we have tried to explain to them! Allow me to share this story. Tom and Erik are two cousins around five and a half years old. They have just seen Erik's baby sister being given her bath and are discussing very seriously the difference between boys and girls. Erik says: "I wonder why girls are not like us?" To which Tom, with great assurance, replies: "Well, you know, girls break everything!" We cannot pursue this even if it is fascinating. Let me simply bring out a point which is important for our purpose.

To develop healthily in their search for meaning, children don't need the way of logical reasoning, but the way of concrete experience and "mystical" or spiritual experience. Children are able to hold opposites together, to see links where we don't. They experience their oneness with all things and bring them together in their own way, through religious imagination, to make sense of them. Maria Harris tells a story about Elise Boulding which illustrates this: "As a child I was told that grandfather spent an hour every morning and evening listening to God. So when I came suddenly upon my grandfather one day seated motionless in his armchair with closed eyes I knew he was not asleep. He was talking to God. I stopped short where I was and stood very still. Perhaps if I listened intently enough I might hear God's voice speaking to my grandfather. But the room remained quiet; not even the faintest whisper reached my ears. After a long time my grandfather opened his eyes, saw me, and smiled at me gently. These moments of intense listening for God's voice in the room with my grandfather are among the most vivid memories of my early childhood."[8] The concrete support was there: the grandfather praying; and the spiritual intuition of God's presence opened the child's heart and mind to a true religious experience much more than would have an explanation on God's presence everywhere. As William Lynch wrote: "The task of the imagination is to imagine the real."[9] This is what the child constantly does with a playful and enchanting freedom, whereas so often we remain stuck to the surface of things.

This completes our brief answer to our first question: What are the main dynamic components of the spiritual embryo in the child? As we have seen, these components are wonderful and powerful energies and capacities which will need loving and lasting care to develop to their full potential. How can parents give that care? This is what we will discuss in the next chapter.

Appropriation to Life

- *What do you think of Francoise's proposal that there is an essential correlation between human eros and spiritual growth?*

- *What are some of the implications for Christian spirituality? For yourself? For those you catechize?*

- *If human desire is essential to the spiritual life, what decision or response does this invite for your own life now?*

Chapter Ten

Helping Parents Be Spiritual Guides for Their Children

Focus for Reflection

The Rite of Baptism refers to parents as "the first teachers of their child in the ways of faith." It then adds, "May they be also the best of teachers, bearing witness to the faith by what they say and do, in Christ Jesus Our Lord."

But rhetoric is cheap! It is so easy to proclaim parents as the primary educators in faith of their children and then give them little or no support in fulfilling their very challenging responsibilities. It is surely imperative now that the Church create networks of support among parents young and old, provide resources and training, invest ministerial personnel and time, and so on, in "nurturing the nurturers."

* *Return to some of your own earliest memories of being nurtured in faith. Pause and dwell on them again for a while.*

* *What do you learn from them now for your own ministry of catechesis? To children? To young parents?*

* *Recall a "religious ritual" of your family from your earliest childhood years. How did it nurture you in faith? What do you learn from it for your ministry today?*

111

> Early childhood education is about
>> sowing seeds of contemplation
> and of love
>> and letting them germinate
> in their time
>> under the gentle touch of the Spirit.

How can we encourage in the home a healthy development of the spiritual embryo in the child? How can we help our children become fully alive spiritually and morally? These are the main questions we will be concerned about in this chapter. But first let us reflect for a moment on the dispositions or attitudes that are needed on the part of the parents if they are to live up to their responsibility. I will mention five. The first one, of course, is awareness. We have described it at length in the chapter on the eucharistic life. It is evident that if the parents are to foster the blossoming of the "contemplative being" in their children, it has to be part of their own experience, of their own being. The second is a faith conviction that the Spirit always precedes us, that she is at work in the child's heart and life—or, as the Catechism of the Catholic Church beautifully puts it, that "God thirsts that we may thirst for Him."[1] The third is true respect for the child's spiritual potential and for his or her way of knowing and experiencing the divine and of expressing his or her experience. The fourth goes even further; it is a willingness of parents to let themselves be led by their children in rediscovering God's presence and God's Reign in the ordinariness of their daily life: "Unless you change and become like little children you will not enter the Kingdom of God" (Mt 18:3). The simplicity, freshness and genuine joy in the child's faith is indeed a rejuvenating treatment for our faith. If we let ourselves be taught by our own children, our "inner child" will perhaps recover this vivid awareness of God's presence in creation, which will allow us to "see the Dancer again" and to playfully join them in the dance of creation. The fifth is an understanding that their task is to sow the seeds and not to reap the harvest. Many months and years will have to go by to allow the seeds to germinate and grow when their time will come under the gentle touch of the Spirit.

So what is the essential task of the parents in the development of the "spiritual embryo" in their children over the first six to eight years? I will describe their common journey in three stages: a joyful concelebration of the gift of life; a gentle evangelization and celebration of God's love; a gentle initiation into a Christian way of life as a eucharistic way of life.

1. A joyful "concelebration" of the gift of life[2]

What does this mean? It simply means taking the time to share as fully and as often as possible in our children's exciting exploration and discovery of their own humaneness, of their body and its wonderful possibilities of enjoyment and action; taking time to share their wonder-filled exploration and discovery of the world around them; taking time to share moments of quiet tenderness and love; and all along enjoying it thoroughly together while we parents celebrate in our hearts and give thanks for God's loving presence as the source of that gift of life. It is also during those early years that the child should begin learning—simply from the way we ourselves behave—the respect and care with which we must treat our environment, all things and living beings around us.

Furthermore I believe it is time for us, when the child is moving on to three years old, to share another basic experience which will be extremely beneficial both for the general development and for the spiritual life of the child. I mean the experience of deep, quiet, conscious breathing and of the well-being, enjoyment and peace it brings to us. The child will enjoy immensely sitting quietly with us to play the breathing-game. At some point we will sense the moment has come to move a step forward, perhaps around three years of age, depending on the child.

2. A gentle evangelization

• *Naming God*

Building on the dynamic components of the spiritual embryo in our children, the longing for happiness and intuitive knowledge of a loving presence at the heart of reality, we will gently begin naming that mysterious presence. The first naming of God is an important moment and we should remember the very wise advice of Maria Harris: ". . . the words we apply to God ought to convey a hesitancy, a tentativeness, and a sense of the impossibility of ever completely naming the Name."[3]

Allow me to describe in very simple language what I feel this first evangelization should be. Remember, this first "content" of the Good News is to be gently shared a little at a time over many months, whenever we sense a readiness, a special moment of awareness in the child.

Someone who loves us very much is giving us this wonderful gift of life, the beauty of the world and each other's love to enjoy. . . . What could we call that Someone? Which words can help us find the names of that Someone? Words like Love, Beauty, Light, Life, Joy?

Maybe we could call that Someone The Beautiful One, The Gracious One, The Powerful One. . . . Yes, and many other names! But there is a very special name we can give that Someone. That name is God. Nobody else can ever be called God. It is a very special and mysterious name, and we always say it with respect and love, because God is so great and life is such a wonderful gift.

We know many things about God, but there are many more things we don't know, and we keep trying all together to know God better all our life long, because God is so wonderful.

However there is one special name of God which helps us understand a little more about who God is, and that name is Love.

Yes, God is love. And there is one thing we know about God which brings us great happiness, which truly is a very good news. This is the good news:

- *God, who is Love, loves us very much.*
- *God, who is Love, is always with us.*
- *God, who is Love, will never turn away from us.*

God loves us so much, so much, that even all the love Mom and Dad have in their heart cannot be as great as the love God has for each one of us.

But Mom and Dad's love can sometimes help us think of God's love. So we can also think of God as the most loving Father or the most loving Mother of all.

Yes, this is good news indeed. Hearing this good news is like finding a precious treasure, or a beautiful pearl.

- *Awakening prayer*

Once God has been named and God's loving presence has been made more explicit, at some point the celebration of our life and our love will become the celebration of God's love, will become praise and thanksgiving through gestures and dance, words and songs, beautiful colors in our drawings or simply moments of silent wonder. Those first moments of contemplative joyful silence we can share with the child are of extreme value for the future development of the child's spiritual life.

As Cavalletti writes beautifully, there is a "kind of connaturality" between the child and God who is Love. And this is a time for the serene enjoyment of God, building deep down in the child a basic trust in God's unconditional love. This is the time when the Spirit gently awakens prayer in the child's heart; but she will need our heart and our voice to educate the child.

These are the years when the child is actively learning his or her mother-tongue. I believe it is then also the time to begin teaching the child, very slowly and gently, our Christian mother-tongue. The first words we use to speak about God or to pray to God should not be "baby-language." They should be inspired by the Bible and the Liturgy of the Church. They should be acclamations or very short simple poetic lines from the Psalms or the Prophets, and it is the contemplative context of our talk or our prayer which will progressively charge these words with rich meaning for the child.

This point is very important because it is this context which will allow the child to "enter religious language rather than merely repeat it or talk about it."[4] Some of those words may be used in sharing with the child moments of "breath prayer." It is with the help of those words, charged with the faith of generations, that the child will little by little learn to express—jointly with his or her own everyday words—the prayer life the Spirit gently awakens in his or her heart over those precious years.

However, very often the child's prayer will not even need words, as a delightful excerpt from Gertrud Nelson's book shows us: "Some years ago, I spent an afternoon caught up in a piece of sewing I was doing. The waste basket near my sewing machine was filled with scraps of fabric cut away from my project. This basket of discards was a fascination to my daughter Annika, who, at the time, was not yet four years old. She rooted through the scraps searching out the long bright strips, collected them to herself, and went off. When I took a moment to check on her, I tracked her whereabouts to the back garden where I found her sitting in the grass with a long pole. She was affixing the scraps to the top of the pole with great sticky wads of tape. 'I'm making a banner for a procession,' she said. 'I need a procession so that God will come down and dance with us.' With that she solemnly lifted her banner to flutter in the wind and slowly she began to dance."[5]

Gestures and dance are a natural way for young children to express their prayer. Often they spontaneously reinvent the liturgical gestures of our tradition, and sometimes they accomplish them with incredible recollection and intensity as well as exuberant joy.

To continue nourishing the child's faith and enriching the child's spiritual experience the parents should be encouraged to use two other means: Bible stories and rituals.

• *Sharing the Word of God*

Carefully chosen Bible stories[6] can be used to awaken in the child basic Christian attitudes through identification with the actors in the stories. Certain parables are also appropriate. Because their symbolic approach stimulates the child's religious imagination, he or she feels free to interpret them according to their present needs to nourish their relationship with God. We should come back to the same stories or parables many times, using a variety of pedagogical means, reading them, telling them, play-acting them with the child. But this should always be done in a prayerful, meditative context, allowing time for the child to express his or her experience in drawing, gestures, songs, rituals, manipulation of objects, etc., and always including some shared time of silence to "think about it in our heart."

It is this context which will little by little help the child sense the difference between these stories and other stories and fairy tales we tell him or her. It will also affirm in our children their capacity for interiority, which is so often lost instead of being enhanced by the way we teach them. All the preceding suggestions of course should apply as much to what is done in pre-school programs.

Jesus obviously will have a very special place in these moments of sharing the Word of God. Jesus will first be presented as the One who came to tell us about God his Father and to show us God's love. A friend and colleague of mine, who had proceeded somewhat along the lines I just suggested for the religious awakening of her children, was amazed one day when her little boy told her: "I wish God would come down or send us someone to tell us more about him!" This was the moment of readiness she took advantage of to introduce Jesus to the child.

One other way of helping the child discern little by little the difference between the Bible stories and other stories is the way we treat the Bible. The book of God's Word should have a special place in the home as in the pre-school setting, and be treated with respect and care; it can become a powerful symbol for the child. I remember with what reverence the children treated the Bible when it was introduced to them in First Grade. Once a little boy made a striking drawing which I can still see. The open Bible was in the center of the page on a bright yellow circle. Rays of light were linking the book to strange little stick people surrounding it; they had huge ears on each side of their heads which made them look like butterflies! When I asked the child to tell me the story about his drawing, he explained everything and said: "Their hearts are full of light because they are hearing the words of God, and you see, they have very big ears so they can listen better!"

Let me repeat what I mentioned briefly in Chapter Six about the importance of short quotations from the Bible to nourish the child's faith. Experience has led me to see clearly over the years how meaningful and life-giving these can become for the children when they are presented in a prayerful, meditative context, allowing the children to truly appropriate them, make them their own; they are truly then "words of life."

I can't resist telling you another story which a young father reported to me. Jennifer was in Grade Two. It was one of those Monday mornings when we wish it was Saturday instead! Daddy was in a bad mood and rushed through the kitchen where Jennifer was having her breakfast without even saying hello. Jennifer quickly got up, grabbed her Daddy's arm and gave him a kiss. Then she said: "Daddy, why didn't you even say hello to me?" Daddy hugged her and said: "I'm sorry, Jenny. I've got problems at work. I'm not looking forward to this day and I just didn't notice you." "Have you said your prayer this morning, Daddy?" "No—not yet," said Daddy. "O.K., come along with me. It will only take a minute." Jenny brought her Daddy to her special prayer corner in her room. She closed her eyes, was silent for a moment and said in a soft voice: "Jesus said, 'Don't be afraid, I am always with you.'" Then she looked up to her Dad: "Just think about that, Daddy, and you'll feel better."

The faith in God's love and God's Word will be especially important when children begin facing what Berryman calls their "existential limits and ultimate concerns." But it is especially true when death comes into the life of the child. What will help the child are not our efforts to try to explain what we cannot really explain. What will help will be our shared faith in God's love and in God's Word, the basic trust which will hopefully have developed in the child's heart, and his or her religious imagination will do the rest. Allow me to develop this a little.

I have always been fascinated by the power of children's religious imagination with its seemingly antagonistic characteristics of anthropomorphism and symbolic intuition. I became even more aware of that when I was doing my experimental research for my doctoral thesis on the children's ideas and feelings concerning death and the after-life. It gave me the privilege to enjoy twenty to thirty minutes of private conversations with more than fifty children between five and nine years old. My point in bringing this up is this: it seems to me that the more we try to explain things, according to our traditional anthropology as if they were simple, the more we mix children up. Let me offer a few examples.

It was a child of eight or nine in France more than thirty-five years ago, who first made me aware of the serious problem we had with that anthropology. The child had had no previous religious education. The lesson taught that when we die our body goes into the earth and our soul to heaven. I remember the perplexed and anguished look on the boy's face when he burst out his question: "But then where shall **I** be?" In the research it was obvious children had the same perplexities: "You told me your grandma was in heaven?" "No, not her, her soul."

A young mother, probably wanting to avoid the word "soul," had told her five year old that our hearts go to heaven, which seemed to upset the child very much. When I asked why, she said: "Well, you know, there will be so many hearts up there, I'm afraid my mom won't be able to find mine!" She obviously pictured valentines stuck all over the sky! The children who were the most serene were those who simply had made their own the faith of their parents or their teachers. For them, being in heaven meant being happy with God forever. As a little girl explained, "We don't really know what it will be like, but it might be like a wonderful feast day that will last forever."

These children did not seem too concerned about the "how," probably because they had their own way of imagining it, which satisfied them for the time being. That need for a word of hope coming from a trusted adult to appease the child's anguish was made painfully clear to me in the same research when a bright and lovely little six year old from an agnostic family said sadly: "My mother told me that when we die we are put in the ground and that's it; it's all over. But I don't want to go in the ground!" And she added: "Do you think I can meet someone someday who will tell me I can live again forever after I'm dead?" I was in a professional situation where I was not supposed, through respect for the parents who allowed us to interview the children, to share my faith. So when the child came back to that question again, I only said that I was sure she would someday meet someone who could tell her that. That little girl and her longing are still in my heart after so many years.

One last word about what I learned from that research. It became evident for me that conversations with children, when we are not trying to indoctrinate them but only to stimulate their own thinking and allow them to express it freely, give them the opportunity to progress and mature in that very process.[7] It is fascinating to see them struggling with anthropomorphic views which they finally reject to move on to a symbolic understanding of the matter. This was striking with the eight year olds when they talked about hell. Here are two examples.

"Some people say . . . I have seen some pictures of hell. But it isn't like that. Because they mean that when you turn your back on the Father when you die, you go to a place you don't know, they mean the Lord Jesus isn't there . . . and then I would say that you suffer so much that you would say it was like being in a fire with a man on fire . . . they call that the devil . . . but that doesn't exist."

"That means that people separate themselves from the Father forever. . . . They have given it a name like that. They say that it is a fiery place, but that means that when you are separated from the Father, it is like a fire. Because it is hard to be separated from the Father forever and never see him; it is like a fire."

I also remember a conversation I overheard between Third Graders early in the year during those precious moments before class begins in the morning when kids freely chat. An Italian boy had brought a picture of hell full of devils and fire: "Daddy gave me the picture and said it was just like that." A bunch of children commented on the picture with more or less skepticism. Some seemed impressed but one boy said very appropriately: "How can he know? He's never been there!" And a little girl moved away, saying: "I don't believe hell is like that. I think hell is in my heart when I don't want to love God."

I was amazed at the deep interest the children manifested in the twenty to thirty minutes of conversation on these austere topics. Many of them said they would like me to come back so we could talk again together. As one girl told me: "You know, it is not often that a grown-up sits down with us just to listen to our ideas. And besides, grown-ups don't like talking about death!"

• *Creating family rituals*

So in this second stage of the child's spiritual development which is a gentle evangelization and celebration of God's love, we can cooperate with the work of the Spirit through the sharing of the Good News, the awakening of prayer and the occasional use of Bible stories and quotes. But we can also use rituals. As we said earlier rituals are an indispensable part of our life, because they allow our vision of faith to get a hold on our daily life. That is why we should help our children from the start to experience and enjoy the basic rhythms of our Christian life, the simple daily rituals of morning and evening prayer, and to discover little by little their rich life-giving meanings. Let's see how we can do that.

— *Daily rituals*

Rituals are a natural part of children's lives. Any baby sitter discovers that, the very first evening. If the bedtime rituals are not respected, this spells trouble! For young children, something you do twice becomes a tradition, and if the third time you forget the order of things and do it differently, you are reproached: "That's not how you make a sandwich!" So let's build on that ritualistic tendancy of the young child.

We know the importance of bedtime rituals and the special tenderness the small child needs at that time to face the insecurity, the vague threat of the night and the solitude. Many parents have the excellent custom of blessing the baby with a cross on the forehead while saying good night. This simple body contact of the gentle gesture on the forehead will become part of the ritual. When the child's awareness of God as a loving presence will be awakened, simple words can accompany the blessing: "God loves you" or "The Lord is with you. Sleep in peace." Happy the child who will thus discover through this simple ritual that we are inseparable from God. I believe this evening blessing had a profound impact on my own discovery of God's presence in my life.

Over the years this brief moment of awareness will gradually become an evening prayer which the child will learn to creatively enrich with our help, and it will probably expand in precious bedtime conversations. Somehow children feel we are more "present" to them at this hour than in the rush of the day, and often their most profound questions come out at this special time, like little five year old Geffry whom I was baby-sitting for a few days. I had told a story, said good night and was leaving the room when he called me back: "Aunt Francoise, tell me, why must everybody die?"

But the questions are not always so "existential," however troublesome they may be for the child. Johnny, four years old, had been very impressed by a cartoon he had seen that day on Noah's ark. At bedtime he seemed concerned and asked: "I really wonder how they got something to eat in the ark; they couldn't go to the supermarket." "Well—there was plenty of water around; they probably went fishing." Johnny seemed satisfied for a second, but then: "No way! There were only two worms!"

In the same way, when the child's awareness of God's love as the source of his or her life has awakened, let us gently invite the child after the morning hug to join us in a simple ritual to greet the day in joy and thankfulness: "Thank you, God, for this new day." Let the children create their own personal ritual; they have wonderful ideas.

Thus the first basic eucharistic attitude, "receiving our life as a gift of love each day," will naturally become part of the child's life. When time will come to prepare for First Eucharist we will gently teach the child to add a gesture of offering to the gesture of praise.[8]

If we can help the child to truly make these simple daily rituals his or her own and enjoy them, and if we continue to help enrich their meaning over the years, linking them creatively to the changing experiences of the child and to his or her increasing religious knowledge, we will have done a great deal to begin helping that child share our experience of a eucharistic life.

Another daily ritual is grace before meals. It can become meaningful if we do not allow it to become routine. The children will see to that if we encourage their creativity and leave them the initiative as they grow up to adapt this moment of prayer to the circumstances of the day or the liturgical seasons. Very briefly let me mention two other types of rituals.

— *Convivial rituals*

As Bernard Cooke writes, "It is important that in Christian families we celebrate the gift of one another, and the gift of experiencing life happily because of our faith that allows us to see God as gracious and loving."[9] A family with a spirit of celebration will find a million occasions for small and large celebrations enriched by family traditions and ethnic customs. This will strengthen the family's love and faith and will keep alive in us our "inner child." As Gertrud Mueller Nelson writes: "Boredom comes from taking for granted what is around us. We are numb. We do not allow ourselves to be touched and quickened. Celebration is like play; it requires something of the childlike."[10]

— *Seasonal rituals linked to the liturgical year*

To celebrate those rituals we should use many natural and biblical liturgical symbols in a contemplative context: light and darkness, water, fire, plants and seeds, icons or statues, clay, bread and wine, incense, etc. Children enjoy greatly mini-celebrations built around these symbols. However we should give at least as much importance to the preparation of a feast as to the feast itself. Indeed it is the waiting, the expectation which will deepen in the child's heart the experience of hope and spiritual desire, allowing the feast itself to keep its "interiority," even in the midst of the "commercial" fuss around feasts like Christmas.

One related point I would like to make is this: although it is important that the child be aware we can pray anytime, anywhere, it is also desirable to have in the home a "sacred place" where we might have the Bible, icons, a candle, flowers, etc., and to decorate it according to the liturgical seasons. The CCC (2691) recommends that every home install a "prayer corner" to induce its members to prayer. Now, what about church?

Many parents wonder if they should bring their children to church during those early years. This is a disputable question. As Robinson's study shows, it can have either positive or negative effects. The "Church God" is not always congenial with the God of the child's spiritual experience. But occasionally bringing the child might be good if the church offers an aesthetic and truly religious atmosphere. The community experience can be meaningful, showing the child that many people outside the family share the same love for God. But if the child does not like it because the church does not offer the ambiance the child needs, it would be better to wait so that the child doesn't learn to resent going to church, as an Anglican minister discovered was the case for his grandson: "Do I have to go, Grandpa? You know, I love Jesus but I hate church."

This brings us to the end of the second stage in the spiritual development of the child. The first stage was a joyful concelebration of the gift of life till around three years of age. The second stage, between three and six, was a gentle evangelization including the first sharing of the Good News, the awakening of prayer, the careful use of a few Bible stories and quotations, and finally rituals and symbols. The third stage, beginning around six, is a gentle initiation into the Christian way of life, which we will describe as a eucharistic life.

But before moving on to that third stage I feel the need to offer a word of caution concerning preschool programs. These can be for the children a wonderful experience if they are conceived and carried out in the spirit of what we have described in this chapter with regard to the spiritual growth of the child. But unfortunately too many preschool programs are not. They are often much too busy, much too pragmatic, concerned with teaching things rather than enhancing the contemplative potential of the child, which is, in my opinion, exactly and only what they should be doing during those precious sensitive years which will never come back.

3. A gentle initiation into the Christian way of life

What we will be discussing now is the moral development of the child. This, of course, is an immense question about which we can learn a lot from many theories of moral development and moral education. Here I only wish to bring out three points of major importance with regard to the Christian aspect of a holistic early moral education.

A) *Avoiding the use of God as a "means" in moral formation*

During the first evangelization period we just described, we are laying the indispensable foundations of the future moral development simply by allowing the child to experience fully, as Cavalletti writes, "the serene enjoyment of God's love." Notice the two words: enjoyment and love.

Christian morality is about love and the search for happiness. For most people, of course, morality is about laws, about do's and don'ts. But genuine Christian morality is about trusting enough in God's love that we accept to search for our happiness in responding to God's invitation to love as Jesus did. I believe with Cavalletti that the more the young child will have had the time and opportunity to "fall in love" with God and enjoy the relationship with God, the better chance there is that the older child's moral response will be "autonomous and genuine." An autonomous and genuine response comes from within the heart where the Spirit of God is active. It is opposed to a fearful and guilt-ridden obedience to an external law imposed by adults often in the name of God.

Of course, right from the start the child must be socialized, learning the need for self-control, discipline, politeness, respect for others, etc. That socialization is extremely important because the basic patterns of relationship in the family will most probably shape the child's future relational attitudes. But parental authority must stand on its own, and we should never use God as a means to get the child to obey or threaten the child with God's displeasure as we often did: "God will get you," "Jesus is crying," etc. When we do that we are distorting the image of God who becomes a "watch-man" God, "the biggest policeman" as a child put it. Is it not true that many of us, older adults, still hide away in our unconscious this "false god" and that our moral life is too often burdened with an unhealthy paralyzing sense of guilt and an unconscious fear, which hinders the development of a healthy and freeing sense of guilt, when we become aware that we have resisted the inner call of the Spirit.

The unhealthy mixture of religion and morals from early child-hood on is one of the causes of the rejection of God by many adults and of many neurotic problems. Let me share with you a few stories to illustrate this. When we were piloting *Come to the Father* we wanted to find out as much as possible about where the children were at when they first began school. So the very first day, before any catechesis, we asked the first grade children if they had heard about God and if they would make a drawing of something which made them think about God (not a drawing of God). Many children drew beautiful things of the world and said God made the world. Some drew Jesus or the cross. Two little boys made quite different drawings. One drew a large face with a big smile on the top of the page; below, separated by a line, were many confusing objects. When I asked the child to explain his work he said: "Here is God, and here are the people burning in hell." "God seems to be smiling," I said. "Yes, God is happy because the people who did not want to obey him are burning in hell."

The other child had drawn three circles: one small circle in the middle, two others on each side, linked to the middle one with a line. He described his drawing as follows: "In the middle it's me," and, pointing to the exterior circles, "this is God and this is the Devil, and they are both pulling at me." One wonders how destructive such images of God can be on the future development of the children.

Just another story to make us smile. Mom has prepared prunes on the dinner table for the dessert. Sarah, four years old, is hungry and eats half of the prunes. Mom comes back and is furious. She puts Sarah in the corner and says: "You stay there now. You've been so naughty, you're making Jesus cry." After a short while Sarah asks: "Is Jesus still crying?" "Of course," says Mom who is not yet over her anger. "Well," says Sarah with a shrug of her shoulders, "if he's still crying, just for prunes, he's only a crybaby!" Thank God for the common sense of children. But this does not help the image of God.

So let us not use God in the early moral education of the young child. Let us also avoid, when evoking the presence of God, to link it to the child's behavior, saying, for instance "God sees everything you do. God is watching you." In one of his books Sartre speaks of his fear of God's glance which prompted him to hide under the table to protect himself from God's eyes. I heard of a Grade One teacher who had over her head a picture of the famous (or infamous) triangle with the eye of God looking at the class. Anytime she had to leave the room for a minute she simply pointed a finger to the picture! God's presence should only be evoked as a loving spiritual presence: "God is always with us because God loves us," rather than "God is everywhere" as we used to say with insistence, which prompted little Denny to look in all the cupboards of the house to see if God might also be hiding there!

B) Encouraging the discovery of different qualities of joy

Building again on a dynamic component of the spiritual embryo, the longing for happiness, encourage the child to search for and experience many different kinds and qualities of joy. First, the joy of discovering his or her special talents and qualities. As Sartre pointed out in the text we cited, each one of us needs to feel he or she is a "signed masterpiece." Developing a positive self-image, a love and appreciation of oneself, is of foundational importance for the child's healthy development.

When little Maria entered Grade One she realized she was very, very small compared to the other children. She was a lovely brunette with fiery black eyes and dark hair, but she was tiny and was upset about it. Whenever she had to draw herself in a picture she always began with the legs which were so long that hardly any room was left for the body. One day we had brought into the classroom a big bunch of country flowers of all colors and sizes. Each child was asked to pick a flower that would represent him or her, so we could make a lovely bouquet which we would put in our prayer-corner during the celebration of the Word as a grateful offering to God for who we are. Maria took a long time to choose her flower. She finally picked out the smallest of all, a slender stalk of forget-me-nots. She came to show it to me and said: "See, it is very small but it is very pretty!" "Indeed," I said, "it is very, very pretty." When Maria came up to put her flower in the bouquet, she was beaming! From that day on she seemed to feel better about herself, and the legs became a little shorter in her drawings!

We should also help the children discover the joy of progressing, of overcoming difficulties or fears, of developing their talents, to reinforce their self-confidence. Children's self-confidence at that age can be severely shattered by the way we treat them, as I discovered with children in Grade One, but fortunately it can also be restored.

Susan and Marilyn were twins. Marilyn was very good at

drawing and enjoyed it very much. But Susan, from the very first day of class, refused even to pick up the crayons when the time came to draw. She was very shy and only said: "No, I can't draw," and sat sadly, hands folded. After a few days I decided to give it another try. I crouched near her little desk and told her I was sure she could draw, and I would be so happy if she would draw for me just a tiny little flower. I asked which color she would like the flower to be. Without a word she pointed to a crayon but did not pick it up. I picked it up for her and offered it. She took it, still without a word. I said: "O.K., take your time. I'll come back later." I walked around the class, talking with other children. Her eyes followed me for a while; then she started drawing for a few seconds and put down her crayon. I went back to her. She had drawn a tiny flower in the bottom left corner of her large drawing pad. I admired the flower—its color, shape, etc. Then I said: "I think that little flower would need some water and some sun to grow." She looked at me, smiled and picked up a blue crayon to draw a few lines under the flower, then a yellow one to draw a small sun at the top of the page. I admired these and said how happy the flower must be, but then I added: "I wonder if she will not feel lonely if she stays alone like that?" I left because another child was calling on me. Susan continued to draw for a long while; then she put down her crayons and looked at me with a smile. I came over again. The whole page was filled with flowers becoming bigger and bigger, from the tiny one on the bottom left to the largest one which filled the whole length on the right side. Susan was radiant. Her self-confidence had been restored after it had probably been shattered by an adult comparing her drawings to those of her twin sister.

Let us avoid however "pushing" the child to be better than everybody else, as some parents do too often to satisfy their own needs. Let the children enjoy their childhood at their own pace.

When we sense the child is ready for it, perhaps around age six depending on the child, let us help him or her discover the special joy of loving, of giving joy to others even when it requires a special effort, or if it is at the expense of our pleasure. Children are indeed capable of seeking and experiencing that special quality of joy. Let me show you what I mean with a story. It is a feast day in Grade One. The Sister Principal comes to the class and gives each child a roll of Life Savers. They must be left on the desk until after the sketches and songs are over. Then Sister says: "O.K., now everybody can enjoy the candies." The children all open their roll and begin exchanging their colors: "I like the red, I like the green. . . . " One little girl, from a very poor family, watches them but does not touch the roll. Sister comes to her: "Hi, Linda. Why don't you eat your candy? Look at your friends. They are all enjoying them." "Oh yes," says Linda, "they are laughing with their mouth now, but tonight, when I share them with my family, I'll laugh in my heart!"

Each experience of the joy we can find in loving, sharing, caring, forgiving, remains in the child as a dynamic force to seek more of them. If occasionally we can bring the child to explicate his or her feelings on that experience, we will help fortify the conviction that we can indeed find happiness in love. We will thus have begun to awaken in the child the second eucharistic attitude, a willingness to give our life and not only live our life. When the child will have experienced that joy often enough, we might tell him or her that Jesus gave us the Law of Love as a way to happiness, and that this is what being a Christian is about: trying to love as Jesus did.

Very soon, of course, the child will become aware that this way of life is difficult to follow. We will then tell the child that we are not alone in this endeavor. Jesus gave us his own Spirit who is always with us to help us to love as Jesus did and find there our happiness. Young children can become very familiar with the Spirit and—perhaps because there are no pictures of the Spirit as there are of Jesus—she can become very naturally a spiritual presence in their heart. Gerry's mother discovered that when he came home from school one day with a drawing: it was an "open house" with one person in each room. Gerry asked: "Mom, do you think these persons are alone in their rooms?" "Yes," said Mom, "they're alone." "No," said Gerry triumphantly. "The Spirit of Jesus is with them!"

C) Using conversations about our life to foster moral development

From around age six or seven we can encourage the child's moral development through dialogues and conversations. But first let me put in a word about communication in the family. Research has shown that during the past twenty years or so, the time allotted to conversations in the family has diminished by 300%. Should we wonder why so many families have so many problems? Even Attorney General Janet Reno in one of her speeches mentioned it: "We have neglected our children in all classes of society. We have no time for them." And she added: "We should free the parents, so they can spend more time with their children." Dolores Curran insists on the same point in her excellent book on family life.[11] Furthermore, surveys of children have shown that the one thing an overwhelming majority of children put at the top of the list, when asked about their most urgent desires, is that parents would spend more time with them.

Communicating is not talking *to* a child, even less *at* a child. It is talking *with* a child, which means listening from the heart, asking questions and accepting questions, sharing feelings and ideas about the experience or the problem so it can be gently, realistically, honestly handled and eventually overcome or lived with. When I talk of conversations in the family about our life, I mean two things: one-on-one conversations which occur more or less spontaneously as daily events unfold or at bedtime; general conversations bringing most of the family together around the kitchen table or elsewhere. Both are needed. Why? First, because those conversations will help our children become aware of the many choices they have to make all day long. They need not be moralizing lectures; they can be quite discreet suggestions.

Meg is a very bright girl who is excellent at spelling. She comes home from school one day and says to her Mom: "We had a dictation today and I had no mistakes. But," she adds mockingly, "Audrey had at least twelve mistakes." Audrey is her best friend. "Wow," says Mom, "that's great for you, but poor Audrey must have felt terrible." "Yeah, she's hopeless at spelling." A week goes by. Meg comes home one afternoon and the same scenario is repeated, but this time Mom says: "Poor Audrey. I'm sure she would really like someone to help her get better." Meg seems startled and says: "But I enjoy being better than she is." And things stay there. Another week goes by, and one afternoon Meg comes home in great spirits: "Hi, Mom. We had spelling again and you know what? Audrey only made three mistakes. The teacher congratulated her and she was so happy!" "That's wonderful," says Mom, "but how come she did so much better?" "Well, I asked the teacher if I could help her during recess to prepare for her dictation." "That was really nice of you, Meg. You were truly being her friend. How do you feel about it now?" "I feel wonderful!" In the evening at bedtime Mom picked up the story of the day and talked it over with Meg to reinforce her awareness of those multiple moral choices we have to make every day and of the special kind of happiness we experience when we make the choice to love.

Yes, we need those one-on-one conversations with our children because it is through loving, open sharing and dialogue that our children will learn little by little to make their own moral decisions and will find the support they need to live up to them in a society which most often does not function in terms of Christian values.

Children are often puzzled and disturbed by what happens to them as they grow up and come up against small and big problems. The first problems arise in the progressive discovery of who they are with regard to others. They have to accept their differences, to appreciate their talents, but also to accept their limitations and shortcomings, so they can be grateful for what they are in spite of those, and learn to appreciate others' gifts and talents.

Problems arise also in their relationships with other members of the family, their schoolmates and neighborhood kids, etc. They have to learn that relationships have ups and downs, that arguing, disagreeing and fighting are part of life within the family and elsewhere, and they have to learn how to get reconciled, to accept responsibility for what they do and to make up, etc. They have to acquire a sense of right and wrong; this discernment is often difficult in our society. The sets of values experienced at home, in school, in the neighborhood, from the media, are very conflicting.

Children today can face great anxieties very early. They might face the problem of losing a friend because they don't want to take part in shoplifting, cheating, or bullying a child because of race or handicap or clumsiness at games, etc. They can themselves be victims of such things. They might have to face the trauma of the breaking up of their family and the readjusting to new members entering the family. To help the children not only survive but grow through all that, we have to help them learn how to interpret their experience in the light of their faith, how to keep their hearts open, their dreams alive, their trust in God's love and their values firm while being realistic. For all that to be possible they need personal spiritual care; they need conversations in which they can share their feelings, their questions, their concerns.

Almost nothing is more urgent and important than taking time to talk when a child is ready to and in need of doing it. Readiness of course is very important; it is useless to try to reason with a child who is all worked up and not capable of listening, as a teacher found out quite bluntly one day. Tony has just thrown a stone at a little girl in the schoolyard. The girl is hurt, and while a teacher is taking her to the infirmary, another one gets hold of Tony and lectures him sternly. Tony endures impatiently. Then the teacher tells him: "Now

I hope you are sorry, Tony." "Yes," Tony bursts out. "I'm sorry, because that's not the girl I wanted to hit!"

So we need one-on-one conversations, when the child is ready for them, to foster moral growth. But we also need general conversations about the family's experiences, moral choices and values. Inasmuch as the children will sense that parents too try to make sense of their lives, to make their decisions in the light of their faith, they will gradually learn to do the same.

If the willingness to give our life and not only live our life is at the heart of a true Christian life, this should come out in the family conversations. They should promote a general attitude of empathy, of compassion which engenders a readiness to become aware of and to respond to the needs of others, to stand up for a cause involving other people's interests, or public problems of pollution, injustice, racism, etc. Whatever is done to respond to those needs or to serve these causes should also be discussed as a family.

For Dolores Curran it is imperative, simply for the health of a family and even more for the quality of its Christian life, that once a week the whole family agree to have a special family meal to really share and celebrate their life together. We know how often our homes are like cafeterias. So there is a strong symbolic meaning in that gathering around the family table on a day chosen by mutual agreement. During the first century the Eucharist was celebrated at the family table. The meal would be special; a favorite dish or dessert might be offered. Everybody would get a chance to share his or her stories of the past week, problems would be discussed in a mood of humor and fellowship, plans for the coming week would be shared; eventually a family ritual might be celebrated. This family experience of sharing can become extremely meaningful for children of all ages. Dolores recalls that when her eldest daughter left for college, this family gathering was one of the things she missed the most about home, so she asked her Mom to put a tape recorder on the table and to send her the tapes even if she was not part of it directly.

This brings us to the end of our reflections on what parents can do to facilitate the spiritual and moral growth of their children during the first six to eight years. Let us conclude this chapter with a last question.

What kind of help do parents need to live up to their responsibility?

This topic would require a whole new book, so I will limit myself to a few suggestions.

Everything we have talked about with regard to laying the foundations for the spiritual blossoming of their children in the first six to eight years has to do with sharing faith in everyday life much more than with teaching religion. However the families we are dealing with today are very different from the good old Catholic families of former days. A great number of them are mixed marriages, single parent families, divorced or blended families. Many are struggling to survive and make ends meet. Many are more or less alienated from the Church, or have never been catechized or evangelized even if they have a basic Christian faith.

Therefore many parents need to be evangelized themselves, so they can discover or rediscover the Good News of God's loving presence at the core of their life, just as it is, with its ups and downs, its joys and hardships. So the most important thing we can do for them is to help them build or rebuild their own relationship with God in the very fabric of their daily life. Then they will start naturally to share their awareness and their faith with their children through moments of wonder, tenderness, joy, and later on intimate conversations about the children's life experiences. That sharing itself will nourish and rejuvenate their faith.

How can we provide that evangelization and that help to the parents? Not by burdening them with programs—remember Janet

Reno's advice: "Let's free the parents so they can have more time with their children"—but rather by reaching out, by getting in touch in a tactful and friendly way to assess their felt needs and see how we can help mainly through warm interpersonal relationships and small support groups. Life is quite difficult for many young families, and it is through this concrete solidarity that they can be evangelized, gently awakened to their spiritual responsibility and supported in their roles over the years. It seems to me that some of the opportune times to do that reaching out in a personalized manner is when young families move into the neighborhood, or when a baby is born, or when parents themselves get in touch with us to ask for their baby to be baptized.

One last comment about this special circumstance. The basic pastoral attitude which is imperative at that time is unconditional welcoming. Whoever they are, wherever they are on their personal journey, the quality of our welcoming, of the relationship we establish with them at that time, is the first revelatory moment in the sacramental process. Let us not burden them with mandatory requirements as if the Church was like a country club for an elite. Rather, let them discover through the warm quality of that first contact that the Church is indeed a great warm family House whose doors are always open to welcome its children whenever they want to come. Then, little by little, one step at a time, according to their personal readiness we can help them rediscover the joy of welcoming God's love in their life and of walking with their children on the wonder-filled paths of the Kingdom which is theirs.

Appropriation to Life

- *What did you learn from this chapter about the place of family rituals and celebrations in the faith nurture of children? What good ideas do you take away from it?*

- *What do you think of Francoise's proposal that the central emphasis of early childhood catechesis should be "enhancing the contemplative potential of the child." Think of some implications for your own catechesis.*

- *Francoise claims that "conversation* with*" each other in the home is imperative for the spiritual and moral well-being of all. Is there a decision that this invites from you? For your catechesis? For your own "home"?*

Conclusion:
Moving On in the
Freedom of the Spirit

Focus for Reflection

Of the three great theological virtues, Christians have placed much emphasis on love *and* faith *but have often neglected the third*—hope. *Yet our very faith in Jesus Christ, and our commitment to be a people of love, both require of us a lively hope. Surely this is particularly true of catechists—our very ministry can be carried on with integrity only if we live in hope. We should also be aware of the insight of contemporary theology that the virtue of hope cannot be an easy trust in God's promises, or an idle longing for better days; we must be ready, with the help of God's grace, to "work for our hopes"—to help to make them come true. With this in mind:*

- *In the context of your faith community, what are some of your own best hopes for the future of religious education?*

- *What are some things that threaten your hopes? That nurture and support them?*

What I have attempted to do in this little book is try to sharpen our awareness of the many positive things that have happened in religious education during this twentieth century, and especially during the last thirty years since Vatican II. I tried to show that in the past ten to fifteen years we have been moving in this great country through a very creative paradigmatic shift toward a more holistic vision of and pastoral approach to religious education. I have also tried to show how we might bring the wonderful energies which are at the heart of that shift to cooperate more decisively and more fruitfully in the coming years. My concern was that the publication of the Catechism of the Catholic Church, if it were misused, might lead us backward. So the suggestions I made were directed to the immediate future.

I will now take the liberty to share with you, very briefly, a few concerns, insights and dreams concerning the long-term future. I will probably not see that many years of the twenty-first century, if any, but while I still can, I would like to do my small part in describing some of the dangers, challenges and opportunities I believe we will be encountering in the long-term future.

It seems to me that we have perhaps, as members of the religious education community, a very special responsibility to speak our mind, to express freely and boldly what we see and sense is happening in the Church which, slowly but surely, might undermine our efforts and compromise the very mission of the Church toward the future generations in the long run. Perhaps we also have a special responsibility to express freely and boldly what changes we feel would be necessary, not only to avoid this slow disintegration but to help the Church acknowledge and welcome the new life which is slowly, secretly, silently awakening in her own womb. The Old Mother Church is harboring new life within herself, but sadly she does not seem ready to welcome it, even to acknowledge it; she seems afraid of what might be born of her.

Amazingly, however, what is slowly, stubbornly taking shape within the Church is also taking shape outside of her. Yes, the old humanity on our planet earth is also pregnant with new life, longing to give birth to a new humanity that would be truly and fully human because it would be reconciled with itself in its twofold essence, the feminine and the masculine, because it would be freed from its demons called greed and domination, because it would claim dignity, freedom and justice for all.

Yes, new life is stirring in the midst of violent pains, in the depths of humankind, because the yeast is in the dough, the Reign of God is at hand, the Spirit and the Logos, the Water and the Fire are powerfully at work. They are slowly penetrating the hearts and minds of human beings from all races and faiths all over the world, giving them the prophetic courage to live and die for that birth to happen. These prophets are sitting together around the same tables, sharing bread and wine, sharing stories of lives and deaths offered for that cause, sharing their dreams for this new humanity which is slowly being born of their blood and their tears, of their hope and their love.

Through our faith we know this is the Body of Christ constantly yearning to be born again in every human heart, in every culture throughout the centuries. Will the Church be part of that cosmic birth and thus be rejuvenated herself? Yes, if she is able to let the Spirit free her from her own fears, from her illusion that she has all the answers, from her own unconscious preoccupation with power and domination. Yes, if she is able to truly be attentive both to the moves of the Spirit and to the signs of the time.

To help her do just that, we from the religious education community should have the simplicity of heart and the audacity to tell her what we would need to see happen in our field of ministry if that new life is to come to maturity instead of being still-born. This is what I will attempt to do. With regard to our educational ministry, indeed to the mission of the Church itself, I would like to bring out three major points. All three have to do with moving on in the freedom of the Spirit.

1. We need more freedom in the Church to ask challenging questions, even on sensitive matters, and to participate in the search for answers.

We should stop trying to fit real life, real people and the Holy Spirit into our categories. We should understand that when we let doctrinal, liturgical or canonical concerns take us over and take precedence over people's real needs and the circumstances of their lives, we become unable to discern both the signs of the time and the gentle touch of the Spirit inviting us to move on creatively to find life-giving answers for new questions and to reorder perhaps our priorities. Let me share with you a simple story which was reported to me recently and which illustrates what I mean.

Saint Anthony's is a lower middle class parish with many young families and very hard-working parents trying to make ends meet. On Sundays very few of them come to Mass, because most of them have a small cabin in the mountains for which they leave late Friday evening or Saturday morning. It is a much needed oasis in their hectic lives, allowing them to share and celebrate their life together, to rest and to relax in the quiet of nature, away from the noise and turmoil of the city. They are "non-practicing" but sincerely believing Catholics. On the occasion of some of the children's preparation for the Eucharist, parents get together and rediscover the importance of celebrating the Eucharist in their community both for them and for their children. But they also feel that the weekend in the mountains is a vital need for their family and cannot be sacrificed. They bring their problem to the pastor and the liturgical team, and together decide that there will be every week a family Mass on Thursday evening. On those evenings the church is full, the families prepare the liturgy together, and the children and teens are happily involved in the preparation and celebration.

The pastor and the liturgical team had two options. They could give priority to maintaining the tradition: Sunday Mass is an obligation, and true Christian families should be able to sacrifice their weekends for it. Or they could reorder their priorities in the light of the parents' questions and needs, and decide that what is important is the spiritual nourishment of those families. We know this question is not only that of St. Anthony's parish. It is a question that innumerable parishes face in the developed countries because the life-style has changed and it will not reverse itself. Could the Church acknowledge that question and propose new guidelines? For instance, the parish community would always celebrate the Eucharist on Sunday, honoring the day of the Lord's resurrection. All those who are able to attend would do so in the name of all; but another special celebration, eventually using the Sunday lectionary if desired, would be offered on a weekday evening for those who cannot attend on Sundays.

Of course, there are many more doctrinal, liturgical or canonical questions which should be raised and addressed. How important it would be for the Church to accept the creative challenge of those new questions and problems which constantly occur in our changing world. And instead of silencing the people who bring them up, or hastening to give authoritative answers, couldn't she call on the people of God to help find the solutions? Couldn't she learn to listen to the "sensus fidelium," to the new ideas of the best scholars, of the mystics and prophets of our time? This, after all, is where the Spirit is at work to guide her. If she does not learn to do that, then I am afraid more and more people will leave her, and our educational ministry to those who stay will become more and more difficult. As we said earlier, quoting Michael Warren, "all persons have a right, indeed a human duty, to become co-producers of religious meaning."[1]

2. There is an urgent need for catechesis to be enlightened and enriched by the most recent research in the interpreting of the Scriptures.

The reform of the Pontifical Biblical Commission in 1971 and the recent publication of the comprehensive document, *The Interpretation of the Bible in the Church,* were indeed a blessing. But in our task as catechists we would need much more precise help as to how the riches of the Bible can truly nourish the faith in ourselves and in our children. It seems to me that one of the areas of research which the Commission encourages would be of special importance for us today: it involves the "continuing dialogue between psychology and psychoanalysis on the one hand and theology on the other. The psychological/psychoanalytic approach to the interpretation of the Bible is part of that dialogue as it is part of a broader discussion within psychological and psychoanalytical circles as to the insights to be drawn from texts of the past."[2]

We have already been greatly helped of course by the historical-critical method and many methods of literary analysis which build on it, by cultural anthropology, etc. But it seems to me that the psychological/psychoanalytical approach which is also linked to the history of religions is one of the most powerful tools for helping us, ordinary Christians, to rediscover the profound and life-giving symbolic meanings of the texts. It is the one, in other terms, which most directly speaks to our heart and our imagination and can move us to deep spiritual encounters with God.

This is why I hope that works like those of the German theologian Eugen Drewermann can soon be translated and published in this country. He is not only a theologian and a philosopher deeply influenced by Kierkegaard, but also a psychoanalyst and a pastor. Using psychoanalysis and the history of religions, building on the critical-historical approach, he goes much further in proposing a symbolic interpretation of the Bible, which has struck a responsive chord and rekindled an incredible interest in theological reflection and spiritual, symbolic reading of the Bible in ordinary people. His books—some of them three or four hundred pages long—are best-sellers. A few have been translated in French, but not yet in English. Not surprisingly he is very controversial and has been suspended by his bishop as professor of religious anthropology at the University of Paderborn, in spite of a petition with 25,000 signatures against the suspension. One need not agree with all his ideas, but what is fascinating is that his way of helping us read the Bible opens up the text and leads us in a profoundly healing, life-giving and challenging world of new meaning.[3] This, I believe, is one of the approaches we will need in the coming years to revitalize the way we read the Bible.

I would like to mention another one which has been recently proposed to us in this country by Bruno Barnhart in his masterpiece already mentioned in Chapter Eight. He invites us to read John "from the center," using an approach which "relies less on methods of scientific exactitude than on intuition and symbolic imagination, inclining less to analysis than to synthesis."[4] He notes that "Western science, in its wonderful development during the past two hundred years, has led us nearly to forget the dimension of depth in knowing . . . of fullness of meaning," and suggests that "A 'postcritical' exegesis might reflect the uncertainty principle of post-Newtonian physics in crossing the frontier of a rigorous precision of particulars into the region of a final depth and intensity of meaning: the most adequate meaning, the great sly fish who is hidden in the whole sea. It would be *a lectio divina,* ancient and ever new, in which, without offense to the literal meaning of the text, the obsessive insistence upon a *single* clear meaning would yield to that glowing field of energy and creative potentiality from which meanings are ever freshly coming forth. The analogy of an energy field is appropriate, for both around the biblical Word and at the center of its materiality lives the creative Spirit, with its inexhaustible plenitude, its living flux of meaning. There is a kind of poetry which is language in movement, living language, word flaming into spirit, and this could probably come closer to the Johannine Word than our prose paraphrases and commentaries."[5]

It seems to me that if we were willing to enter more deeply into these symbolic, spiritual approaches to the Bible we would perhaps become able to re-express the doctrinal truths of our faith in a more poetic, existential and symbolic language which would be much more understandable to people and touch their hearts the way beautiful paintings, poems or music can do.

3. We need the Church to reconsider her decisions for an all-male, all-celibate clergy if we are to prevent a eucharistic famine in the next century in many parts of the world.

As we said earlier the Eucharist is at the heart of Christian life, because it is a mystery of communion with God, with one another and with all of creation which is pervasive to our whole life and to the history of humankind. But even if it is the daily living of that mystery of communion which is essential, its communal ritualization in the eucharistic celebration is of paramount importance and must be available to all who wish to celebrate it as often as they want. Is this not one of the major pastoral reasons why the Church should rethink both the way she celebrates the Eucharist and who presides over it?

Hopefully the Church will be more and more made up of small communities, of families coming together to share the Word, share their faith and support one another. Wouldn't it be wonderful if they could also celebrate the Eucharist and share the Bread of Life in communion with the whole Church? After all, it would only be returning to what was in the beginning.

But it seems to me it is all the sacraments which should be reinterpreted in the context of today's circumstances and in the light of the new insights coming from theological and biblical studies. All this would be of great importance and value for our ministry in religious education.

Much more of course should be said about what would need to be done for the Church to better fullfill her mission in the twenty-first century, but it is not the purpose of this little book. Let me finish simply by sharing a few thoughts and dreams from the heart.

If the Church allows the new life which the Spirit has awakened in her to be born, she will herself be rejuvenated, revitalized. Because she will let go of many cumbersome things which were hiding the deepest mystery of her being, she will become herself more and more: a living sign of the Kingdom, a wellspring of living waters, the living sacrament of God's gracious love offered to all. She will become more and more the prophetic, mystical and convivial community which we all dream of and which the world so badly needs.

What can we do to help that birth happen? I think we should let loose our imaginations and our dreams in the great wind of the Spirit, and rich, powerful images of the Church will awaken in our hearts. Some very ancient ones will reappear in our consciousness, new ones will come to life, and if we share them and let them shape our lives and our ministries, wonderful things will happen; as a great prophet of our time, Helder Camara, told us once, "When we dream alone it is only a dream, but when we dream together it is already the beginning of a new reality."

Yes, let us move on in the freedom of the Spirit, and let us rejoice and give thanks with Paul for new beginnings: "To him whose power now at work in us can do immeasurably more than we ask or imagine—to him be glory in the church and in Christ Jesus through all generations, world without end. Amen."[6]

Appropriation to Life

- *Francoise calls us to "let loose our imaginations and our dreams in the great wind of the Spirit."*

  Pause for a few moments and let this happen as you think about the future of the Church, of our society, of our world. What images and dreams emerge for you?

- *If you were to choose one overarching "lived" response that you might make to reading this book, what would it be? Will you "let it be"?*

Notes

Introduction

(1) When the controversy about the masculine connotation of the word God started some years ago, I wondered why this did not really bother me. Then I became aware that it was probably because I had always unconsciously given to the word Spirit a feminine connotation just as I had given to the word God a "fatherly" connotation. So I decided to use the feminine for the Spirit as the Hebrew word "ruah" suggests and to continue using the masculine for God as Father. This is, for the moment, my way of overcoming the language problem about God.

1. The Rich Legacy of the Past

(1) *Handing on the Faith* (Herder and Herder, 1959). It had been translated in French a few years earlier.

2. An Important Paradigmatic Shift

(1) *Catechetical Renewal Network,* 1993.

(2) In *The Living Light* (1992, vol. 28, n. 2) Richard Reichert wrote a very challenging article entitled "Catholics Confront Ecclesiological Schizophrenia," in which he addresses this issue. He rightly

149

points out—speaking from his long and rich experience—that for more than twenty years catechists have been struggling with two problems: first, an "ecclesiological schizophrenia" whereby too often local churches were functioning on a pre-Vatican II ecclesiology while the catechists were trying to work in the spirit of Vatican II, and, second, an "unequal partnership" whereby catechists were all alone trying "to provide all that is implied in the words message, community and service," while parishes and families were not doing their share.

3. The Theological Foundation of the New Approach

(1) *L'histoire des hommes, récit de Dieu* (Cerf, 1992), p. 15.

(2) Ibid., p. 20 (my translation for all excerpts from this book).

(3) Ibid., p. 17.

(4) Ibid., p. 179.

(5) Ibid., p. 180.

(6) Ibid., p. 181.

(7) Ibid., pp. 181–182. Also cf. Marcus J. Borg, *Meeting Jesus Again for the First Time* (Harper, 1994), p. 55. This remarkable and challenging book brings us to the core of what believing in Jesus and following Jesus' way really means in the light of modern biblical scholarship.

(8) Schillebeeckx, op. cit., pp. 55ff.

(9) Ibid., p. 183.

(10) Borg beautifully concludes his book in stressing the difference between being conditioned into "believing things about Jesus" and believing in Jesus, which means "to give one's heart, one's self, at its deepest level, to the post-Easter Jesus, who is the Living Lord, the side of God turned towards us, the face of God, the Lord who is also the Spirit" (op. cit., p. 137).

4. The Need for Structural Changes

(1) "Catechists Confront Ecclesiological Schizophrenia," in *The Living Light,* vol. 28, n. 2 (1992), pp. 166–175.

(2) Ibid., p. 170.

(3) Ibid., p. 171.

(4) Ibid., p. 169.

(5) Ibid., p. 167.

(6) J. Brennan, *Re-imagining the Parish* (Crossroad, 1990).

(7) Ibid., p. 38.

(8) Ibid.

5. A Theoretical Outline of the Overall Religious Education Journey

(1) Some authors criticize the use of this word in Christian ministry because they feel—and rightly so—that *pre-evangelization* is already a way to evangelize. I agree with them that it is in fact a

first step or phase in the evangelization endeavor, which I characterize as evangelizing by our deeds, by the quality of our relationships with people. However I use it here because it is shorter and simpler than "first phase in evangelization."

(2) "But Will They Ever Come Running?" *The Living Light*, Spring 1993, pp. 45–51.

(3) Ibid., p. 49.

6. The Concern for Religious Literacy and Curriculum Design

(1) How interesting it would be if the Religious Education Department of a University could set up a multi-disciplinary team including religious educators, psychologists interested in religious development, Bible scholars, theologians and liturgists, who would try to tackle the question in initiating a longitudinal research!

(2) USCC, 1994.

(3) See Gerard Sloyan's article "The Role of the Bible in Catechesis According to the Catechism," in *Introducing the Catechism of the Catholic Church,* edited by Berard L. Marthaler (Paulist Press, 1994). Also the excellent 1994 Fall issue of *The Living Light*, especially articles by Raymond F. Collins, John Gillman and John J. Pilch.

(4) Ibid., p. 15.

(5) USCC, op. cit., p. 33.

(6) Gerard Sloyan, op. cit., p. 36.

(7) We know that the fundamentalist approach to the Bible is a major problem for our time, but this is also true of the esoteric approach which can lead to incredible aberrations. One only needs to turn on the TV to become aware of the problem, but many of our Catholic Christians, both adults and young people, are almost defenseless against these trends.

(8) "Youth Evangelization and Counter-Evangelization" in *The Living Light*, vol. 30, n. 1, pp. 42–52. This article offers a remarkable and challenging analysis of the present situation.

(9) See in particular Sections III and IV.

(10) "Beyond the Literal Sense," by Joseph Jensen, in *The Living Light*, vol. 29, n. 4, p. 56.

(11) *Education Under Siege* (Bergin and Garvey, 1985), p. 51, quoted in *The Living Light*, vol. 30, n. 1, p. 47.

(12) Ibid., pp. 47–48.

(13) Ibid., p. 49.

(14) Ibid., p. 50.

(15) Tom Groome himself states that in a charming real-life story in *Sharing Faith*, op. cit., p. 149.

(16) See an interesting article about this whole process in *The Living Light,* Spring 1991, vol. 27, n. 3: "Observe, Judge, Act: A Method of Discovery and Formation That Worked," by Mary Irene Zotti.

(17) Maria Harris, *Teaching and Religious Imagination* (Harper, 1987). See in particular pp. 159–63. This marvelous book is a foundational resource for all who teach catechists.

(18) Trinity Press International, 1993.

(19) *Sadhana, A Way to God. Christian Exercises in Eastern Form* (Doubleday, 1984).

7. *Adult Education, Evangelization and Religious Practice*

(1) *Sacramentum Mundi,* 2:311, quoted in "Socialization as a Model for Catechists," by Berard Marthaler, in *Foundations of Religious Education* (Paulist Press, 1978).

8. *The Place and Role of the Eucharist in a Holistic Vision of Religious Education*

(1) Bruno Barnhart, *The Good Wine: Reading John from the Center* (Paulist Press, 1993).

(2) Of course, what John puts in this long soliloquy is probably a kind of meditative summary of his memories about many of Jesus' sayings during his whole life. But the very fact that it was put there, after the washing of the feet and the eucharistic ritual which the other Gospels relate, seems to me profoundly significant.

(3) I cannot give precise references to some of Tony's quotations because they come from the notes I took when I had the privilege to experience a week's retreat with him two years before his death.

(4) The profound and powerful meaning of this simple ritual can be richly enhanced if it is understood in the context of Teilhard de Chardin's beautiful meditation called *The Mass on the World.*

9. The Awakening of Faith and Longing for God From a Psychological Perspective

(1) This crucial stage of development has been analyzed by Donald Winnicot in fascinating detail in his last work *Playing and Reality* (London, Tavistock Publications Ltd., 1971). Jerome Berryman very clearly summarizes Winnicot's ideas on this topic in his recent book *Godly Play.* Here is an excerpt: "The newborn infant is an unconnected set of feeling states and impressions. The mother holds the child in her mind as well as in her arms to give form to this chaos by bathing, cooing to, naming, rocking, feeding, changing and all the other things that mothers do with babies. The mother, Winnicot suggested, has a special intuition that can anticipate what the baby needs. This lasts some weeks or even longer until the mother's own needs begin to take over again. The baby does not need perfection. During this time the baby needs good enough mothering. The newborn senses a need such as the desire to be fed. The child imagines the satisfaction of the hunger and at the same time the mother has intuited the child's needs and feeds her baby. As a result the child experiences a sense of omnipotence, a magical joining of desire and satisfaction. It is this sense that gives the child a sense of 'me,' a sense of reality. The illusion begins that there is an external reality that corresponds to the infant's own capacity to create. When the mother's period of special sensitivity to the child's needs begins to wane, the satisfaction of needs lags. After all, the child has de-

manded almost all of her life in the service of his or her development. Frustration begins for the child. The gap between desire and
satisfaction widens. Out of this disillusionment a sense of 'not-me'
arises. The mother is out there, independent of me, the child experiences. The mother becomes an object. Reality is taking shape in
terms of its subjective and objective aspects" (Jerome W. Berryman,
Godly Play, A Way of Religious Education (Harper & Row, 1992),
pp. 10–11.

(2) A. Vergote, *The Religious Man, A Psychological Study of Religious Attitudes* (Pflaum Press, 1990), p. 161.

(3) Ibid., p. 33.

(4) Edward Robinson, *The Original Vision: A Study of the Religious Experience of Childhood* (Seabury, 1983).

(5) Gertrud Mueller Nelson, *To Dance with God* (Paulist Press,
1986). This book is very special, written by a mother who is also
an artist and a deeply spiritual person who studied with Jung in
Switzerland. I recommend it to all parents.

(6) A. Vergote, op. cit., p. 163. See also Rumke, *The Psychology
of Unbelief* (London, 1957) as cited by Vergote.

(7) As cited in A. Vergote, op. cit., p. 163.

(8) Quoted in *Family Ministry,* edited by Gloria Durka and Joanmarie Smith (Winston Press, 1980), p. 66.

(9) William F. Lynch, *Images of Hope: Imagination as Healer of
the Hopeless* (Helicon, 1965).

10. Helping Parents Be Spiritual Guides for Their Children

(1) CCC, art. 2560.

(2) Sofia Cavalletti, *The Religious Potential of the Child* (Paulist Press, 1983). This book is a must for all who are interested in early childhood.

(3) *Family Ministry,* edited by Gloria Durka and Joanmarie Smith (Winston Press, 1980), p. 62.

(4) Jerome Berryman, op. cit., p. 65.

(5) Gertrud Mueller Nelson, op. cit., p. 3.

(6) Thank God, Ronald Goldman's influence has decreased in recent years, at least in this country. When he published his book *Religious Thinking from Childhood to Adolescence* (Routledge and Kegan Paul, 1964) he discouraged many educators from using Bible stories with children, except in an anecdotal way, pretending they were not able to grasp their symbolic meaning. Concerning this topic, Gertrud Mueller Nelson shared with me another amazing story about her little girl Annika. Annika had to pass an interview with the Director before being accepted in a pre-school program. The Director asked Annika if her Mom told her stories, and what kind of stories. Annika said that her Mom told her stories from fairy tales and from Greek myths. Surprised, the Director asked: "Do you know what a myth is?" After a moment of silence Annika said: "Yes, it is a story which is not true on the outside but is true on the inside!"

(7) This became even more obvious to me when reading a wonderful book called *The Spiritual Life of Children* by Robert Coles (Houghton Mifflin, 1990).

(8) I have prepared a colorful leaflet proposing simple morning and evening rituals which might help the child and the parents at this time to discover and enjoy the eucharistic dimension of our daily life. It is called *Together with Jesus* and is available at St. Anthony Messenger Press, Cincinnati, Ohio.

(9) *Family Ministry,* op. cit., p. 192.

(10) Ibid., p. 26.

(11) See *Traits of the Healthy Family* (Winston Press, 1980), and *Stress and the Healthy Family* (Winston Press, 1985).

Conclusion:
Moving On in the Freedom of the Spirit

(1) Michael Warren, op. cit., p. 50.

(2) Raymond F. Collins, "Hearing the Word," in *The Living Light,* vol. 31, n. 1, p. 5.

(3) The following are some of Drewermann's books already translated in French:
• *La parole qui guérit* (3rd edition) (Cerf, 1992).
• *L'essentiel est invisible. Une lecture psychanalytique du "Petit Prince"* (3rd edition) (Cerf, 1993).
• *La Peur et la Faute (Psychanalyse et Théologie morale,* tome I) (Cerf, 1992).

- *L'Amour et la Réconciliation (Psychanalyse et Théologie morale,* tome II) (Cerf, 1992).
- *Le Mensonge et le Suicide (Psychanalyse et Théologie morale,* tome III) (Cerf, 1992).
- *L'Evangile de Marc. Images de la rédemption,* tome I. *Introduction* (Cerf, 1993).
- *Dieu guérisseur. La légende de Tobit ou le périlleux chemin de la rédemption* (Cerf, 1993).
- *De la naissance des dieux à la naissance du Christ* (Editions du Seuil, 1992).
- *Fonctionnaires de Dieu* (Albin Michel, 1993).
- *Le Progrès meurtrier* (Editions Stock, 1993).
- With the Dalai Lama: *Les Voies du coeur. Non-violence et dialogue entre les religions* (Cerf, 1993).

Also, Drewermann's *Discovering the Godchild Within* (Crossroad, 1993) is now available in translation by Peter Heinegg.

(4) Op. cit., p. 2.

(5) Ibid., p. 15.

(6) Eph 3:20.